2017

Circumstance
Copyright © 2017 Wicked Publishing.
First Edition
Published through Wicked Publishing LLC 2017
This is a work of fiction. Names, characters, places and incidents are the product of the author's imagination or are used fictitiously. Any resemblance of actual persons, living or dead, business establishments, events, or locales is entirely coincidental.

This book, or parts thereof, may not be reproduced in any form without permission

Credits
Editor: Jess Bennett
Cover Design by Shiralyn Lee

ISBN-13:M978-1546449331
ISBN-10: 1546449337

Dedication

Circumstance is dedicated to the memory of David John Paull, my Blood Brother and best friend, always.

1983 - 2015

Acknowledgements

This book came about when I became the unofficial cheerleader of Ronni Meyrick after I read her book, *Hero*. I loved the book so much, I pestered her, along with her publishers, to write a sequel. What I didn't realise then was that every action has a consequence, and after Ronni agreed to write her sequel, Shiralyn Lee challenged me to write a book of my own! Given that I'm not one to run from challenges, I immediately said yes, setting myself on a wild and exciting road that led to the birth of *Circumstance*. I soon realised that I knew absolutely nothing about writing a book, but with the help of Dawn Carter and Shiralyn Lee of Wicked Publishing, and also

Ronni Meyrick (we are now known as the Terrible Twins!), I've learned quickly! Thank you for taking a chance on me and giving me the opportunity of a lifetime.

Many thanks go to the friends, family, and colleagues who've either egged me on or helped me with technical information. In no particular order, thank you to: WPC Claire Wilding for her expertise in police protocol and what would happen in certain legal situations, and Jackie Longdon for pointing me in the right direction on some aspects of mental health management. My good friend, Frank Horner, for being my biggest cheerleader when editing has threatened to overwhelm me, and my mother, Jean Charlton, the strongest and most inspiring woman I know. I wouldn't be who I am if it wasn't for you.

Biggest thanks, as always, must go to my partner Karen, who takes everything in her stride and believes in me no matter what I take on. No one else would sit and trawl through the mental health act with me and roll around on the floor late into the night plotting fight scenes until we're both bruised and battered. I love you.

CIRCUMSTANCE

<u>**Chapter 1**</u>

Wheels screeched against the tarmac as the plane landed and pulled Helen Kennedy from the dark thoughts that had plagued her since she'd boarded. She took a deep breath. *I've finally made it*, she thought as the doors opened towards passport control. All she had to do was clear through security and pick up her luggage, and then she'd be on her way to beginning the process of rebuilding her life after losing her wife to cancer.

Throwing her carry-on bag over her shoulder, she made her way across the tarmac; the stench of jet fuel and the evening humidity made it hard for her to breathe. It was a relief to find that the limo driver she'd hired was waiting just outside the glass door. Her journey was almost complete.

Once in her suite, she opened the balcony door and stepped out. She inhaled the salty air. She closed her eyes, and for the first time in months, she felt at peace. Her stomach rumbled, which reminded her she hadn't eaten all day. Letting out a moan, she took a step backward and took one last deep breath before closing the door. As much as she hated eating in hotel restaurants, she had no choice. It was that or grab a burger from a drive-through, and she'd worked too hard to maintain her athletic figure. She took one quick glance in the mirror and combed her fingers through her short blonde waves. The corner of her mouth inched up slightly. *I look as tired as I feel.*

Her mood instantly changed when she glanced at the urn on the bed. She had more important things to do than eat. Picking up the remains of her past, she rushed from the room.

***

Urn in hand, Helen walked along the shore. The moon's reflection shimmered across the ocean. The breath-taking scene would normally have made her happy, but not now. The beach at Akti Kanari was the place Helen first dropped to one knee and proposed, all those years ago. They'd even toyed with the idea of coming back to this beautiful Greek beach to get married, but in the end, they did it in England. The memory of her wife looking so beautiful and radiant in a simple pale blue dress as she'd said her vows crippled Helen with a fresh wave of heartbreak. If only they'd known how short their time together would be.

Circumstance
Kate Charlton

Standing firm upon the boulders, she opened the lid and sprinkled some of the ashes in her hand. This was goodbye. She'd lost everything that meant the world to her in a single moment.

"I love you, Meg," her words punched through her sob. She dropped to her knees, her tears mixing with the ashes as she cast them into the swelling waves. She watched as they flowed on the surface of the water. For a second, it almost looked like Meg's silhouette was waving farewell. Helen smiled until the form dissipated under the current.

***

Helen woke with tears streaming down her face, the sheets tangled around her body and every inch of her drenched in sweat. She fought to calm her breathing. Just a nightmare. Just the same damned nightmare that had tormented her for the past year. Throwing the sheets off her body, she climbed out of bed, crossed the room, and opened the minibar fridge. Naked, she sat out on the balcony and sipped her whisky, letting the sounds of the ocean soothe her soul. The warm breeze brushed over her skin. She sighed deeply. *Is this nightmare ever going end?* All she wanted was her life back.

Circumstance
Kate Charlton

Chapter 2

After releasing Meg to the ocean, Helen holed herself up in her room for days until she thought she'd go insane. Had her wife been there with her, Helen was well aware that she'd have given Helen a piece of her mind and forced her to get a grip. It took all of her willpower, but Helen finally dragged herself from her bed, showered, and left her room that morning. As jarring as it felt to be surrounded by so many people again after her own enforced solitude, she realised it was the best decision she'd made.

Helen loved nothing more than people watching, especially when they were engrossed in their own conversations. She stretched her tanned legs out in front of her. Pursing her lips, she leaned back and exhaled. *This is the life! Year-round hot weather, the sea, an abundance of sand to walk through bare-footed, and, well, who knows what else I'll find when I embark on my solo adventure.*

She took a sip of her ice-cold ouzo and spotted a lone woman seated at a table toward the end of the patio. She looked tired and on edge with a glass of red wine in her hand and the remains of a small dinner pushed to one side in front of her.

Helen looked for signs of a companion, though everything about her and the props in front of her suggested she was alone. *Interesting*. She let her gaze wander over the full lips, bright eyes, and aquiline nose that gave the perfect face a hint of lopsided character. The tanned, toned body also suggested this stranger took good care of herself.

Listening to the hubbub of the other guests sitting around their tables, conversing in French, German, Swedish, and a smattering of English, she took pleasure in trying to pick out words. Tonight, though, she kept finding her eyes drawn back to the brunette.

After another scan of the room, she tapped a cigarillo from the box on the table and popped it between her lips. She paused before lighting it and looked down at the vintage Colibri lighter in her hand. It had been a gift from her father when she made partner in her first GP practice almost twenty years ago. Practicing medicine gave her purpose, but she'd never thought about death until she lost Meg. It was a sudden realization that she wasn't invincible. She eyed the glowing ember of the freshly-lit smoke and stubbed it out in the ash tray. Lighting them was sometimes more of a habit than a desire. She felt suddenly weary and acutely aware that she was alone, despite being surrounded by strangers. *If I look over and she's still there, I'll introduce myself. If not, it's time for bed.* Taking a deep breath to steady her nerves, Helen glanced back at the table where the mystery woman had been only a few moments ago. A sense of relief and a slight sadness she couldn't explain gripped Helen's stomach when she found the table now abandoned except for an empty, perspiring wine glass. She smiled wanly and picked up her things. *It's definitely time for bed.*

***

The sun caressed Helen's skin as she lounged in her patio chair, a cigarillo in one hand and a double espresso cooling in front of her. She loved the way the early morning sun shimmered on the swimming pool. The water gave off an ethereal glow as it bounced off the tanned bodies of the die-hard sun worshippers already soaking up the rays at eight thirty in the morning.

Her peace was suddenly shattered as someone jarred her chair from behind and a cold glass of juice spilled over her shoulder and into her lap. Chaos ensued as she jumped up, trying to swipe off as much of the sticky liquid as she could. A husky female voice cut through her surprise.

"Oh, Jesus! Shit! I'm so bloody sorry. I'm an idiot!"

Circumstance
Kate Charlton

Helen broke into laughter and looked up into the green eyes that belonged to the dark-haired stranger she had admired from afar the night before.

"Here, let me help you. I feel terrible. I've just bloody drowned you in juice, for goodness sake!" She thrust a handful of limp paper napkins at Helen, her face wrought with panic.

"Hey, it's okay. Accidents happen," Helen said as she directed the woman to a chair. "Really, it's okay. The shorts cost me a fiver and I think the top was about two quid. They'll both wash and I have a case full of spares."

The brunette's features finally softened, and the invisible marionette strings that had been holding her upright snapped as she slumped in her chair and covered her face with both hands.

Helen couldn't make out whether she was laughing or crying as she waited for the woman to speak. Slowly, the hands slid from her face and a small smile pulled at the corner of the full mouth.

"Not the most perfect start to my day. I guess I didn't get near enough sleep last night. I hope you'll let me pay for the laundry service to take care of those." Her voice trailed off as she glanced into Helen's eyes and she quickly looked down. "Here I go being rude again. My name's Kathy Harland and I'm so sorry for ruining your morning."

The woman's modulated tones made Helen's stomach flip-flop in a way it hadn't done in a hell of a long time. She coughed several times before she could speak.

"It's fine. Drink your coffee, calm yourself down, and join me for breakfast, yes? Unless you're waiting for someone?" Helen knew it was a blatant probe, but it was a good a way to learn more about her cool companion.

Kathy pursed her lips, as though trying to formulate an answer that wouldn't bring too many questions. "No, I'm not waiting for anyone."

Breakfast was long and relaxing as the two women made light conversation over courses of coffee, fruit, and sweet Greek delicacies. They shared little details about themselves, how long they'd been on the island, and how long they were planning on staying, though Kathy was still reserved. Helen had never been one for women who played hard to get, but there was something about the nervous ice queen that made her want to scratch the surface of that tough exterior. *Way to go, Kennedy*, she thought as she regarded Kathy with a sideways glance. *Pick the hardest woman in the place to focus your damned libido on.*

Circumstance
Kate Charlton

The only time Kathy seemed to open up was when she confided how she had wanted to run and hide when her flip flop had caught on the leg of the chair, sending half of her beverage sailing through the air. She admitted how relieved she'd been when Helen had laughed.

"Well, I might have had a different attitude if the assailant was a big burly guy with a beer gut and a handlebar moustache." Helen winked and paused for a minute, appreciating the smile that lit up her new-found friend's face. "Look, I don't know if you have any plans today, but it can get a little boring spending it alone sometimes. Would you like to come up to the port with me this afternoon, see if we can get out for a little joy-ride?"

Kathy bit her lip and looked down at the table. Her hands knotted in her lap, and Helen's stomach dropped. Had she moved too fast?

But Kathy closed her eyes, took a deep breath, and smiled.

"Sure, I'd love to."

***

The day had gone better than planned. It had been so long since Kathy had interacted with a stranger, much less held a full conversation with one. Kathy's first instinct had been to say no without giving the offer any real consideration. She'd learned to mistrust strangers so much these days that she tried to avoid them in social situations, but she'd quite literally fallen into Helen Kennedy's lap. She was thousands of miles from home and probably safer than she had been in quite some time.

She had no idea why, but she instantly liked Helen and appreciated when she led the conversation, allowing Kathy to lull into an easy silence between brief and unimportant chit-chat. That gave her a chance to formulate topics, but her mind kept wandering back to why Helen was there alone. She seemed far too attractive to not have an admirer or partner on her arm.

The intrusive thoughts alarmed her. She had enough going on in her life without finding a stranger sexually appealing. Besides, she didn't even know if this woman was gay. She laughed inwardly. *Who am I kidding?* Helen set her gaydar off big time, with her silver thumb ring and the hint of an interlocking female symbol tattoo poking out of the shoulder strap of her top. She wondered if she was being subtle as she observed Helen's profile. She had obvious crows' feet around her eyes and mouth, but it only added to her beauty. Her slightly crooked Roman nose and the mole above her left eye made her face beautifully imperfect – a landscape that could be explored for hours. They'd had such a perfect day together, sailing in the ocean just outside the bay and sunbathing on the bleached deck of the boat they'd hired for the afternoon. For two strangers, they seemed to find unusual comfort in long silences, without needing to speak or ask each other a hundred and one "getting to know you" questions. Having dinner together on their return to the hotel seemed like the obvious thing to do and Kathy didn't have to think twice about it.

As they sat together, sharing drinks and a light meal, Kathy caught herself and a wave of panic rose in her belly. She couldn't do this. She refused to let herself fall blind into a situation that would let anyone get that close to her again. She stood fast, pushing her chair back with a loud scrape, threw her napkin down on the table, and excused herself as she darted away from the table towards the restaurant behind them.

***

Helen sat stunned. This was the second time in a few hours that she had crashed in and out of interactions with Kathy. Wiping the corner of her mouth with her napkin, she gazed over at the stairwell, not quite comprehending what had just happened. They'd shared such a perfect day together and it felt as though it'd all evaporated in a puff of smoke. Following Kathy wasn't an option. She didn't know her room number and Helen couldn't be sure that she wasn't to blame for her new friend's sudden disappearance.

"Damn it all to hell!"

She stared at the remains of her meal and felt her stomach lurch. Without a second glance in the direction of the stairs, Helen left the table and headed towards the bar. If she couldn't quash her frustration, she could certainly try to drown it.

***

Helen opened her eyes, a pool of sweat forming between the curves of her breasts. With a towel clinging to her chest, she sat up and looked around. It had been two days and Kathy was still nowhere in sight. She had no idea what she'd done to chase her off, but there was no way that woman was going to ruin her vacation.

Once she had changed into dry clothes, she threw on her cap and took herself out in the direction of the old town. She'd been visiting Rhodes for the past six years – always the same hotel, always the same faces. She loved the familiarity of the place, the friendliness of the locals, and the gentle pace of life. It was a wonderful way of decompressing from her job as a GP back in Newcastle. She loved her job, but a busy medical practise made for a busy life.

Circumstance
Kate Charlton

She ambled through the narrow-cobbled streets of the medieval town, dancing around throngs of tourists who were desperate to spend their hard-earned euros in the myriad gift shops, clothes shops, and bars that crammed the winding streets. She made her way towards the top of the walled town, to the café-bar that she'd frequented since she'd started to holiday here.

Her friend Ianis leaned beside the chalkboard that advertised beer for two euros and cocktails for three. He shifted from one leg to the other. When he saw her, his dark brows furrowed, and then a broad smile brightened his swarthy features. He held out his arms.

"*Kalimera*, my friend!" He pulled her into a warm bear hug, his damp shirt stretching across his ample stomach.

Helen allowed herself to be led to a table and listened as Ianis shouted into the back of the café for two double espressos and a plate of stuffed vine leaves. "You here alone this year, my friend?" he asked as he lit a cigarillo for her and a cigarette for himself.

Helen inhaled deeply as she tapped the ash on the side of the ashtray. "I am, indeed. This is my thirty-ninth birthday gift to myself. I think it's what Meg would have wanted."

Circumstance
Kate Charlton

Ianis's thick black eyebrows knitted together in a frown. "My English may not be perfect, but, past tense, Helen?"

Helen's eyes clouded, and sadness crept into her voice. "I lost her three weeks before Christmas, Ianis. The cancer came back. She died within two months of the diagnosis. I think she'd lost the will to fight it for a third time."

The big man reached across the table and squeezed her hand tightly as a tear slid down her cheek. Coming back alone was one of the hardest things she'd ever done.

Circumstance
Kate Charlton

Chapter 3

Silence occupied the space around Kathy. She hadn't realized how secluded she'd been until spending that short time with Helen. And she knew she'd been rude, and most probably looked a little bit crazy when she ran off with no explanation. She felt comfortable around her new friend, but also vulnerable, and that was something she couldn't deal with. No matter how relaxed she was, her nerves were still rattled.

And it was all thanks to the bastard who'd been stalking her, whoever they were. Even though she'd changed her number, the threatening messages in the middle of the night continued, and the dark shadow outside her bedroom window had become more frequent. But by the time the police arrived, the person was always gone.

She'd taken the stairs two at a time instead of the lift to get to her room on the fourth floor faster. It was at times like these she struggled to breathe. Nothing she'd done in the past calmed her, and today was no different. With her back against the door, she slid down and pulled her knees into her chest. Tears built and streamed down her face, leaving trails in her foundation.

Circumstance
Kate Charlton

A tap on the door made her jump.

"Room service," a female voice called out.

"Can you do it later?"

"Yes, ma'am," the voice replied.

"Wait," Kathy called out. She needed to pull herself from the self-induced state she'd spiralled into, and this was the perfect opportunity to shake the dark mood. She stumbled to her feet and opened the door. The woman was already on her way down the hall, but swiftly turned around. Kathy apologised and allowed the maid to enter her room. "I just need clean towels, that's all."

The maid took two plush white towels from her cart and headed straight to the bathroom. She removed the used towels and when she left the room, threw them into the laundry hamper and made her way to the elevator. Kathy clung to the door and watched her go until she was out of sight. She blew out a long, slow breath, forcing out the remains of her nervous energy. She couldn't hide away forever.

***

It had been sixteen months since she'd broken up with Anna, and Kathy didn't know whether she found it liberating or terrifying. Being single again meant that she didn't have to put anyone's needs above her own anymore and she could come and go as she pleased, but she missed the companionship of a steady partner, someone she'd grown with and loved for so long. That thought alone made her chuckle mirthlessly. Anna's betrayal had made her question everything she thought she knew about relationships and then some.

She relaxed on a pool float. The water rippled around her, causing her to bob slightly, but her peace was broken when a wave of water splashed over her. She pushed herself upright, coughing, ready to give the idiot a piece of her mind as she wiped the chlorine from her eyes. But before she could speak, her gaze was drawn toward familiar blue eyes.

"Hello," she choked out.

Helen's perfectly shaped eyebrow rose as she grinned at the slender woman before her.

"Hi, there."

Silence filled the space between them. Just as Kathy was ready to speak, Helen pulled her into the centre of the pool. "Water polo's about to start. Would you like to take part?"

***

Circumstance
Kate Charlton

The game was fast and furious, since the young German guys playing with them took the match seriously. Kathy was dunked under the water more than once and found it strangely liberating to scrabble with complete strangers, roughhousing in a way that she hadn't since she was a kid.

By the time the game was over, she realised that she was laughing as Helen helped her out of the pool. *Laughing,* she thought. *I haven't done that in quite some time.*

"So," Helen began as she roughly towelled herself dry. "You think we can be friends for the duration of this holiday, or have I disgraced myself enough that you want to avoid me for the whole two weeks?"

Kathy smiled without looking up, worried that her eyes would give away the attraction that had been building within her.

"If you can manage to behave yourself, I think it might be nice to have a holiday companion," she said shyly.

"Me, behave myself?" Helen repeated with mock-indignation. "It wasn't me who threw a perfectly good glass of juice over a stranger then bolted from the dinner table all in one day." Her tone was teasing, but Kathy still felt her shoulders tense. Helen winked. "I'll behave, I promise."

Kathy forced herself to relax.

"I'm going to weigh twenty stone by the time I get back home if I don't restrain myself," she joked, her attention wandering to the trays of chilled deserts at the other side of the restaurant. There was no fighting the inevitable; her legendary sweet tooth lead her to the fancy pastries.

"With a figure like yours, I'd doubt that. It's obvious from looking at you that you work out, and as far as my professional knowledge goes, salad is not a danger food for weight gain."

"Maybe not, but white wine at two-thirty in the afternoon might be," Kathy grinned, then pointed to the selection of low-calorie choices on Helen's plate. "Tell me about yourself?"

Helen arched her eyebrows and took a gulp of her wine. "What would you like to know?"

Kathy shrugged as she speared an olive with her fork and popped it into her mouth. "Well, all I know is your name, and the fact that you're a crap diver. So, fill in the blanks for me."

Circumstance
Kate Charlton

"Well, I turned thirty-nine a few days ago, I live and work in Newcastle, I'm a general practitioner, and I'm here alone. No children, and very gay. Me in a nutshell." Her eyes roved across Kathy's face.

"You're here alone? Does that mean you're single or that you're merely holidaying alone?" She didn't understand why she'd picked up on that piece of information over the rest Helen had offered, or why she wanted to know so badly.

"Both, I suppose. I'm a widow. My wife had breast cancer and died last year. She'd battled it twice so bravely and beaten it both times. The third time…" Helen's voice cracked.

"I'm sorry. I didn't mean to upset you. We can change the subject," Kathy quickly added.

Helen sighed, her gaze falling to the tablecloth as she lowered her head, shaking it slowly. "No, it's okay. The third time, it came back aggressively and it was at stage four by the time she was re-diagnosed. She died within two months. I felt so helpless. I'm a fucking GP, for God's sake! I know some of the best consultants in the Northeast and I couldn't save my own fucking wife." She paused and looked out of the huge windows, staring out to the ocean. "I wasn't myself for a few months after she passed, and I ended up taking sick leave. Then I spent a lot of time in denial and drank a lot of whisky, which, of course, didn't bring her back or make me feel any better. If it hadn't been for a good friend who pulled me back from the brink of self-destruction, I don't know how I would have ended up."

She fell silent, and Kathy couldn't bring herself to say anything.

"What about you? Tell me about you," Helen asked, straightening in her seat.

Kathy's brain suddenly went into self-preservation mode and she had to fight the urge to bolt again. *You're being ridiculous*, she chastised herself. *This woman's only making conversation. Isn't that what new acquaintances do, get to know one another?* She took a deep breath and began, "I'm a forty-two-year-old solicitor specialising in publishing and copyright law, and I live and work in London—gay and here alone." Her answer was clipped and guarded.

"Do you have a partner or anyone special in your life?" Helen enquired, mirroring Kathy's interest.

"I thought so."

Circumstance
Kate Charlton

Chapter 4

Kathy perched on the edge of her bed, her phone clutched tightly in her hand. "I promise, I'm okay. I got here safely, but I had no reception, so I wasn't able to call until now."

"I was worried you'd decided to do a full bunk and drop off the face of the earth!" her friend Michael chastised.

"No, Mike, I'm fine. I'm sorry it took me so long to check in, but I promise," she reaffirmed, "I'm fine."

Michael breathed a heavy sigh into the phone. *"Anna came by yesterday."*

The words hung in the air and Kathy felt her blood run cold. Her fingers moved to her throat and she toyed with the silver locket around her neck that had belonged to her mother. She'd give anything to have her here; she'd always known what to do in any situation.

"Are you there, Kath?" Michael asked.

"I'm here. You didn't tell her where I was, did you?" her voice trembled like a butterfly on a breeze.

Circumstance
Kate Charlton

"Of course not. I didn't even let her over the doorstep. I told her I wasn't getting involved and to stay away from my house and from me. She knows better than to come back again."

Kathy knew that Anna wouldn't stop looking. It wasn't in her nature to quit. She sighed deeply, trying to calm her breathing. *How long can I keep running?*

***

On the other side of the hotel, Helen lay wide awake, her arms thrown across her eyes as she willed sleep to come, but she was fighting a losing battle. She loved spending time in Greece and she loved this hotel, but in years gone by, Meg would've been lying beside her, enjoying the experience. Their last time together was bleak. Helen had stayed by her side in a darkened room where the smell of death hung in the air. She could still picture her wife's hand in hers, the once youthful skin reduced to translucent, sinewy claws. Meg's face remained beautiful until the end. Even though her cheekbones jutted beneath pale skin, her smile never faded. Helen wouldn't have admitted it at the time. It was a strange relief when Meg took her last breath, but at the same time she couldn't let go of her hand. It'd felt as though her own heart stopped right then and there—an overwhelming pain that radiated through her chest and escaped as an agonised roar. Everything after Meg died had become a blur. Twelve months later, the loss still clung to her.

After another hour of failed sleep, Helen rolled to the edge of the bed and pulled herself up. She had limited choices. One was to drink herself into a stupor, and the other was to go for a late-night swim. With a forceful thump, she slammed her hand down on the nightstand. "Pull yourself together, Kennedy. Meg wouldn't want you to wallow in self-pity."

***

Helen jumped into the pool feet-first. The water cooled her hot skin and she welcomed it.

"I see I'm not the only one who couldn't sleep," a voice called out from the hot tub.

She didn't have to turn around to know who had spoken. "I would have called your room, but I thought you'd be asleep."

"Sleep is a concept I forgot a long time ago."

That was something else she and Kathy shared. Sleep hadn't been a friend for a long time.

"How about a few laps with me?"

"How about you join me in the hot tub and we'll order a bottle of wine?"

Her pulse raced.

"Wine, hot tub and a beautiful woman. Boy, a girl couldn't get any luckier."

"Was that a yes?"

Helen grinned. "Absolutely."

***

The sun crept into Kathy's room, casting what looked like a flashlight beam upon her bed. She looked at her watch and a smile stretched across her face as she sat up. It was almost evening. She'd slept through most of the day. Just last night, she and Helen relaxed by the pool until daybreak. Before they went their separate ways, they agreed to meet for dinner, and from the beeping on her phone alarm, she only had an hour to get ready.

***

Kathy let Helen walk her back to her room that evening after a shared dinner of squid, olives, sardines, and garlic bread, though Helen declined the offer of fried *marida* when she realised that these were eaten whole. Helen was chivalrous in an old-fashioned, soft butch kind of way, and Kathy was surprised at how safe she felt with her.

"Would you like to do a day trip tomorrow?"

Kathy considered her options and laughed. She had no plans. "Yeah, I think I'd like that. What did you have in mind?"

"I was thinking of a boat trip out to the island of Symi. It's something I've done every year since I started coming here. It's beautiful and I think you'll love it. We could catch the boat out from the harbour in the morning."

Kathy brushed her wavy hair back behind her ear, a habit she had when she was considering something. Her eyes flicked to Helen's full lips.

"Sure, that sounds great."

Helen smiled broadly. "Great! Be ready by seven-thirty. I'll knock for you and we can head straight out after breakfast."

"I'll be ready. Thank you for a great evening, Helen. I had a good time."

Kathy gently shut the door, but she thought she heard Helen whisper a soft goodnight of her own as she ambled away down the corridor.

Circumstance
Kate Charlton

***

On the deck of the catamaran, Helen and Kathy sat side-by-side as the sun burned against the delicate skin of their necks despite the early morning hour.

Helen shifted in her seat. *Boy, she looks damned cute in that floppy straw hat and those Jackie O sunglasses.* It wasn't until that morning that it occurred to her: she'd developed a crush on Kathy. At first, she'd felt guilty, and she rationalized that it was normal since she'd just released Meg's ashes. But the guilt still found a home in her chest.

"Your back's starting to go red. Want some cream on it?" she asked.

Kathy looked out at the water. A small muscle twitched in the corner of her mouth, almost imperceptible.

"Is this good medical advice, Doctor?" she asked.

Helen arched an eyebrow and played along. "Absolutely. Skin cancer is a big deal, and you're certainly more susceptible when you blast your skin with rays for a week or two after being covered up for the other fifty weeks of the year. Pass the cream, turn around, and be a good patient."

Circumstance
Kate Charlton

Kathy did as she was told and gasped as Helen's fingers touched the hot skin across her shoulders and slid beneath the thin fabric of her vest top, then up over her shoulders and neck.

"Your turn." Kathy spun in her seat, facing Helen. "Turn around."

"I like it when you're forceful," Helen teased and let out a hearty laugh. It was funny until Kathy's delicate fingers brushed over her skin, causing a tingling sensation to shoot between her legs. Her brain scrambled to decide whether the reaction was due to the cold cream on her hot skin or the physical contact of an attractive woman's hands. She was sure of one thing: she didn't want Kathy to stop.

The boat ride took a little over an hour before the harbour town of Gialos came into view. Kathy was rendered speechless at the beauty of the place. The red-roofed houses climbed steeply up the horseshoe hillside, like a scene from a classical painting. She reached for Helen's hand.

"My god, it's beautiful. I've seen some places, but this…" her voice trailed off.

Circumstance
Kate Charlton

She sounds like a kid who's just opened her best Christmas gift ever. Helen squeezed the hand that held hers. "Come on, time to explore."

***

They found a café on the corner beside the dock and as soon as they entered, they received a warm welcome from the waiter, who led them to comfortable upholstered seats. They sat side-by-side as the young Greek man took their order.

"I'll have a red wine, please," Helen stated.

"And for your girlfriend?" the waiter asked.

The women looked at each other and laughed awkwardly, but neither bothered to correct him.

Chapter 5

Heat flushed through Kathy's cheeks. It had been a long time since she'd been interested in another woman, as she'd been with Anna for so many years. It made her feel strangely elated. She couldn't stop herself from grinning. It actually brought to mind her first school-girl crush, when she was infatuated with her English teacher. That crush lasted for almost two years. Needing to put a little space between her and Helen, she picked up their empty glasses and walked back to the bar. She ordered a piña colada for herself and another margarita for her companion. After taking several deep breaths, she returned to their table, then took Helen by the hand without saying a word and led her to the dance floor.

"May I have this dance?"

Helen smiled shyly. "I thought you'd never ask."

***

Later that evening, Helen's eyes flew open and her gaze darted around the room. She was in bed, alone. She sat upright, her skin damp with sweat. *Damn it*! To calm her thoughts, she took a few deep breaths. Lust infused with a tingling sensation had ensnared her. It'd been so

Circumstance
Kate Charlton

long since she'd felt this turned on, and she needed release. She slid her hand down over her taut abdomen to the growing wetness between her legs and closed her eyes, seeing images of both Meg and Kathy. Her fingers slid with ease over the swollen mound and as she stroked the delicate skin, tension built until the orgasm reached the surface and exploded, sending shock waves throughout her body. Then she lay still, basking in the sensation of small aftershocks of pleasure tugging inside her.

***

Lying on the sunbed by the pool, Kathy realised that she really liked Helen. In the few days she'd known her, everything that had been normal had changed. She rolled the word 'ex' around in her head and said it aloud to hear how it sounded. Anna was her ex. Ex everything. *Is Helen a rebound crush?* she wondered. *What constitutes a rebound after all?* It had been a little over sixteen months since she'd collected her things from the apartment whilst Anna was at work and moved in with Michael and Paul until she could figure out what the hell she was going to do with her life.

Helen walked up the steps on the other side of the swimming pool, with a newspaper in one hand, a lit cigarillo in the other, and large sporty sunglasses protecting her eyes. "Good morning. I missed you at breakfast."

With a half-smile, Kathy waved her hand, gesturing for Helen to sit.

Helen slid easily into an empty chair and stubbed her cigarillo out in the ashtray. "I didn't sleep too well last night, so I went for a long walk early this morning. I love to sit on the beach and watch the sky change colours as the sun comes up. It's like watching an invisible hand painting a portrait."

"You have a wonderful way with words." Kathy laid the book she was reading down. "I don't have that gift with words unless I'm arguing a case in court, and I'm sure no one thinks it's very poetic."

"What are you reading?" Helen asked, picking up the book in front of Kathy.

"*1984*. I found a copy on the bookstand downstairs. I remember reading it years ago, when I was a student. It terrified me then, and it still does now. Have you read it?"

"Years ago. Orwell wasn't too far off the mark! Big Brother is definitely watching us all!"

As if by magic, the waitress, Althaia, appeared with a double espresso and set it down in front of Helen.

Circumstance
Kate Charlton

"You look like you need the pep-up this morning." She winked and disappeared as quickly as she had come.

That was a little personal. Surely she didn't spend the night with the Greek waitress? Kathy shook the thought from her mind and told herself it was none of her damned business what Helen did, or whom she did it with.

She made herself smile. "I've reserved us a couple of sunbeds if you're interested in improving your tan."

***

"Lie on your belly and I'll rub some lotion onto your back before you burn." Kathy's sultry voice held a tone that meant Helen wasn't allowed to argue.

Like a scolded school-child, she did as she was told and tucked her arms under her head like a cushion. She could feel Kathy's slender fingers rubbing the cool lotion over every inch of her back and under her bikini straps. *Dear God, the woman's turning me on!* Kathy's hands moved lower, to the small of her back, sliding just below the hem of her bikini bottoms. Helen stiffened, embarrassed at the arousal she was feeling.

"Stay still," Kathy instructed her. "I need to get under the material so you don't have a burn line!"

Circumstance
Kate Charlton

When Kathy was finished, she reclined on her own sunbed.

"Tell me something interesting about yourself?" Helen asked as she relaxed, soaking in the bed's rays.

Kathy peered over the top of her glasses. "Define interesting."

Helen tapped a cigarillo out of the box and slid it between her thin lips. Her long fingers palmed the lighter and lit the tip.

"Well," she began, blowing a plume of smoke above her head. "I know nothing about you other than your age, profession, and where you live. Do you have siblings? Parents? What do you do for fun in the real world?"

"I'm an only child. My father's still living; he's a retired lawyer who practised family law. Mum passed away eight years ago from a sudden brain aneurysm. She fell to the floor while cooking dinner one evening and just never woke up. She was only fifty-nine."

"I'm sorry," Helen replied gently and brushed her hand over Kathy's knee.

The moment was broken when a waitress appeared with a tray of fruit kebab to cool them down.

Kathy bit into a piece of pineapple, the juice running down over her chin. Helen couldn't help but laugh. She reached out with her thumb, wiping it away.

"Would you like a bib?" she teased, raising her eyebrow.

"Smart arse," Kathy winked.

"Come on, what do you do for fun?"

Kathy thought for a moment. "You know what, this may sound really pathetic, but I don't really do anything for fun! I work long hours, and on weekends, I have transcripts and god knows what else to catch up with. I don't suppose work events and client dinners really count, do they?"

"Nope!" Helen chuckled. "We really need to get you out more." She winked again, slowly this time, enjoying the blush that crept over Kathy's sun-kissed cheeks. *She's cute when she blushes.*

"What about you, Doc? What do you do for fun?"

"Well, I play bass guitar in a rock band, believe it or not. We're all GPs and we've had the band since uni. We still do gigs. I also play Sunday league football."

Circumstance
Kate Charlton

Kathy tilted her head in consideration, her tongue sliding over her bottom lip. "Does your band have a name?"

"Don't laugh. We're called Dry Bones. It's really original for a group of middle-aged rocking GPs, eh?"

Kathy laughed and swatted at her.

"Can I take you out to dinner tonight?" Helen asked gently.

Kathy regarded her for a minute, her eyes narrowing, "Are you asking me out on a date, Doc?"

Fuck it. "Yeah, I suppose I am."

"I'd like that, Doc."

Circumstance
Kate Charlton

Circumstance
Kate Charlton

Chapter 6

Kathy stood in front of the bathroom mirror and applied wine-red lipstick to her full lips. Her brunette waves scrunched into loose curls, which seemed to develop naturally in the Greek humidity. What felt like thousands of butterflies fluttered in her belly. She was going on a date with Helen, who knew nothing about her life and the craziness that had resulted in her being here. She took a deep breath, knowing she needed a pep talk.

"I hope you're at home," she muttered to herself as she dug her phone out of her purse.

The phone rang three times before Michael picked up.

"Glad you're still alive, sweetie!" he joked. *"To what do I owe the pleasure?"*

"I've got a date!" Kathy blurted without pause.

"Wow! You go, girl! A little holiday romance never did anyone any harm. Is she a gorgeous Greek mama who wants to blow your mind the Mediterranean way?"

Kathy laughed and found herself relaxing. "No, she's an English GP who's on holiday out here too."

Circumstance
Kate Charlton

Michael giggled like a school-boy revving into full camp mode. *"Tell me more!"*

"Tall, blonde, athletic, wise face, and a body to die for. Old fashioned chivalry and a sexy smile."

"Baby, you had better make sure to put on your sexiest, laciest undies, because she will be peeling them off with her teeth!"

"Mikey!" Kathy couldn't hold her giggles at her friend's blatant one-track mind. "Seriously, though, do you think I'm doing the right thing? I only left Anna a year and a half ago and my life is one fucking enormous drama!"

"Baby, listen to me. Anna has put you through hell for the last few years of your relationship. She could've put a stop to it all, but she didn't because she's a coward! Get yourself out there, have an amazing time, and let this sexy doctor wine, dine, and woo you. Do you hear me?"

She knew her best friend was right, and Mike knew her better than she knew herself most of the time. He and his husband really were her rocks, and she didn't know what she'd do without them in her life.

***

Circumstance
Kate Charlton

A familiar perfume filled the air. Helen turned on her heels when Kathy came into view. She wore a flowing white summer dress, the late evening sunshine highlighting the gold and red streaks in her hair.

"Stunning," Helen said softly, holding her hand out for Kathy.

Kathy took Helen's arm, wrapping her fingers around the muscular bicep covered in an elegant white shirt, and together they walked slowly down the narrow streets until they reached the entrance of the restaurant.

Ianis, Helen's friend, stood in his usual spot next to the blackboard and grinned broadly. He called out his usual greeting and pulled each of them into a bear hug.

"*Kalispera*, ladies! Welcome! Is this a date, Helen?"

Helen blushed as she introduced Kathy to her boisterous Greek friend, who then led them to the best outdoor table. Helen loved the man for his good nature and constant smile. She and Meg had spent many evenings sipping ouzo with him in years past.

"*Ena lepto!*" he called over his shoulder.

Helen took Kathy's hand in hers, stroking her thumb over the smooth skin. "This is a perfect place to eat and watch the sunset."

Circumstance
Kate Charlton

"It's beautiful," Kathy agreed.

They looked down over the narrow-cobbled street, the sun a huge ball of orange fire hanging in the sky before them.

"It's breath-taking. The sunset happens so quickly here, but what a sight to behold."

Before Kathy could reply, Ianis reappeared with a bottle of champagne and two glasses. "This, ladies, is for you, and with my compliments. Two beautiful women." After pouring them a glass each, he left them with menus to choose their meal in peace.

***

Kathy leaned back in her seat and patted her stomach. "I'm stuffed. I really couldn't eat another bite."

Helen grinned. "I told you, Ianis does the best seafood on the whole island. I've sampled plenty enough to know." They sat in comfortable silence for a few minutes, letting their meal digest whilst sipping champagne. "When we first met, and I asked if you had anyone at home, you said you thought so. Will you tell me what that meant? Because I really like you, Kathy, and I know that's crazy after a few days. I guess I just need to know if I'm just a holiday fling or whether you'll let me call you when we get back to Blighty."

Circumstance
Kate Charlton

Kathy took a deep breath. She knew Helen was right and did deserve an explanation regarding her situation.

"I'm single," she said. "I walked out on her a little over sixteen months ago and I am never going back. She betrayed me in ways I never thought possible. I wouldn't blame you if you went running for the hills knowing that. I'm going through a mountain of shit right now."

Helen took Kathy's hand in her own and kissed her palm. "I'm not going to run."

Kathy excused herself to use the bathroom, leaving Helen to contemplate the new information she'd been given.

Ianis slid into a seat beside her, his girth filling the narrow space.

"She's a beauty, yes?" He smiled.

"Yes, Ianis. She is. I just keep asking myself what I'm doing. It sounds like she's got some serious shit going on and I keep getting pangs of guilt over Meg."

Ianis held Helen's lighter to the cigarillo she'd slipped between her lips. "My friend, Meg isn't here. Where she is, she can't come back from, but I know that if she could, she'd be telling you to live your life and be happy. She adored you, Helen, and she would be so unhappy if she knew you were agonising over living your life. She would like your new friend, no?"

"She really would, Ianis. She'd say that she was a gentle soul and a good match for me. Can I handle the baggage, though?"

Ianis shrugged. "Only you know the answer to that. A word of caution, though, don't let it put you off until you know all the facts. We all have baggage. We all have trying times. If you really like her, support her."

Ianis stood when Kathy reappeared.

"Time for digestifs!" he announced and headed back into the restaurant.

***

The night air hung thick, but the cool breeze kept them from becoming over-heated as they walked back to the hotel, arm-in-arm. Helen felt pleasantly tipsy from the constant drinks that Ianis had plied them with. By the time they reached the entrance, she felt lighter. She was glad Kathy told her about the break-up, and, more importantly, that there was no one at home waiting for Kathy.

"Nightcap?" she asked as they walked up the front steps and into the lobby.

Kathy stopped and turned to face her.

Circumstance
Kate Charlton

"Your room or mine?" she asked huskily.

"Lead the way." Helen gulped.

They hurried up the stairs to Kathy's floor. Helen's heart raced. She felt like a teenager sneaking out for her first midnight tryst.

The door to Kathy's room closed behind them with a satisfying thud, shutting out the rest of the world. Without invitation, Helen turned Kathy around, wrapped her arms around Kathy's slender waist, and brushed her hair away from her neck. Hungrily, her lips met the soft skin just behind Kathy's ear, her nostrils filling with the scent of pink pepper, jasmine, and patchouli.

Kathy gasped. Her hands covered Helen's and she pushed her back against Helen's chest.

"Do you want me to stop?" Helen whispered hoarsely.

"No."

Helen's hands moved up her body, cupping her breasts through the thin fabric of her dress. Her nipples instantly became hard and erect. Helen's tongue licked hungrily over her throat. Pulling away, Kathy spun around and threw her arms around Helen's neck, their lips meeting with a desire Helen never knew she possessed.

Circumstance
Kate Charlton

Helen pulled at Kathy's dress, sliding it up over her hips, then over her head. Her breath caught. Even though she'd seen Kathy in a bikini, she looked incredible in matching lace underwear.

Kathy smiled shyly as she reached for the buttons of Helen's shirt and unfastened them one at a time until the white fabric slid to the floor. She kissed the exposed flesh as she pushed the trousers down so that they pooled around Helen's feet.

"You're so god-damned beautiful," she breathed. Kathy's pupils grew large, her eyelids closed slightly with emotion and desire as she accepted another deep kiss, Helen's tongue sliding over hers.

Quickly, the pair discarded their underwear and eased onto the bed in a tangle of arms and legs, hungry for every inch of each other.

Helen then rolled Kathy onto her back and straddled her hips, marvelling at the white flesh that had been covered by her bikini. She reached for Kathy's nipples, rolling them between her fingers and thumbs until Kathy moaned with pleasure.

"Don't move!" she purred, then jumped off the bed. She heard Kathy groan. She grabbed a silk scarf draped over the chair and returned to the bed. "Hands above your head."

Kathy did as she was told and let Helen tie her wrists to the headboard.

"Please, take me!" she gasped.

Helen moved down Kathy's body and sucked a nipple into her mouth; her hot tongue flicked over the tip as her teeth grazed the base. With her free hand, she reached down between Kathy's open legs and lazily trailed a finger over the wet centre.

Kathy moaned.

Helen slid down the length of her lover's body until her face was only inches away from Kathy's smooth centre. She ran her tongue up the inside of her thigh, nipping with her teeth every so often, eliciting small whimpers from the woman who was unable to move below her. She loved how aroused she was making her, knowing how desperate Kathy was becoming by the growing wetness between her lips. Slowly, deliberately, she ran her tongue over the hard clit before pushing her tongue between the folds and inside, forcing a long, guttural moan from Kathy's throat. Then she replaced her tongue with two fingers, using her mouth to tease Kathy's swollen clit. She pulled her fingers out and brought them to Kathy's lips, then rubbed them over her soft tongue, causing her own juices to soak her thighs as Kathy pulled them into her mouth.

It was more than Helen could bear. She needed to come, but she didn't want to do it alone. She pushed two fingers back into her pussy, her thumb working the throbbing clit above. She lay the length of Kathy's side and kissed her deeply as her orgasm built. Kathy cried out just as Helen's climax washed over her, one, then two, until the third exploded, causing her body to convulse, and at the same time, their hips collapsed.

Tears washed over Kathy's cheeks as Helen untied the silk scarf that held her wrists. "That was…That was..."

"I know. It was."

Chapter 7

Sunlight streamed through the balcony door. Helen opened her eyes and gazed down at her torso—the white sheet tangled around her hips on one side and Kathy draped over the other. She let her eyes wander over the contours of the sleeping woman in her arms. She was awed by every curve, ever scattered freckles on her chest, even the tiny scar below one collarbone. *You're one lucky bastard, Kennedy.*

Her cheer faded as she reflected back on the dream she'd had. Meg had stood before her with an angelic expression. She no longer looked sick. As she spoke, her trademark crooked grin lit up her gentle features perfectly. In the dream, she stroked Helen's fringe away from her eyes, as she often had in life. *"I love you. You need to be happy, Hels. Everything will work out, you'll see."* And with that, she'd gone.

Tears welled in her eyes. The dream felt so real. She thought back to what Ianis had said about how Meg would want to see her happy and hoped that the dream was a small sign of that truth. She felt a stirring beside her and let the image of her wife dissolve from her thoughts. The woman beside her was alive and needed her right now. She pressed herself against Kathy's back and kissed the freckled shoulder.

"Good morning, you," Kathy sighed in a sleepy, smoky voice. She rolled onto her back, her arms pulled high above her head, her belly taught as she stretched like a languid cat in the sun.

"Did you sleep well?" Helen asked, resting on her elbow so she could see Kathy better.

Kathy yawned and winked slowly. "Better than I have in a long time. How about you?"

Helen pulled her in close. "Better." She kissed her, revelling in the sensation of warm, inviting lips.

***

They spent the next few days exploring the island and all it had to offer. Sitting at the foot of the doe statue at the port of Mandraki, they sipped on iced coffees and watched cruise ships and fishing boats pull into the port.

The sun bouncing back from the water's surface gave the surrounding area an ethereal glow that didn't exist outside of the Mediterranean Islands, and as they walked along the dockside, Kathy was awed by fishing boats that had been turned into floating seashell shops. The shells they sold were made into wind chimes and wall hangings.

Circumstance
Kate Charlton

Pearlescent pinks and whites decorated the fishing vessels as if they'd floated in from a magical land. Their sails sang the songs of the ocean as they whispered in the breeze.

Her favourite trip had been to Lindos, with its chalk-white buildings nestled at the base of an enormous hill. At the top stood the Acropolis: the jewel in the town's crown. The climb had been hot and hard with the sun beating down on their backs, but the view across the bay had more than made up for it.

At the inner ruins, the women stood hand-in-hand, gazing out over the red-tiled rooftops, tiny church, and bluest ocean. Their nights were spent wrapped in each other's arms, making love and getting to know each other better. It was as though the cares of the world had washed away.

Every time they discussed returning to the UK, Helen repeatedly told Kathy not to worry. They'd figure out how they were going to see each other.

Even though Kathy believed Helen, she still felt uneasy. Her feelings for Helen had grown, and it scared her. She'd never been as wrapped up in Anna or craved her as much as she did Helen. She wasn't sure why. *I wonder if it's the events of the past few years that soured my view of our relationship? No, that's not it. Helen just*

Circumstance
Kate Charlton

seems to have the innate ability to touch parts of my soul that no woman has before. But she knew if they were going to have a relationship, she needed to tell Helen everything about herself and what she'd been experiencing.

***

A slight breeze blew over the patio of the hotel's restaurant. The entertainment team were having a night off, so it was easy to make conversation. That was something Kathy wanted, but would need Dutch courage to do.

She cleared her throat. "There are things about myself I've not told you, and I need you to let me talk and get everything out in the open, Helen. When I'm finished, I'll answer all your questions, but please, just let me get it all out first."

Helen nodded slowly.

"Okay," she replied, and lit a cigarillo.

Kathy inhaled and began. "I met Anna twelve years ago at a party held by mutual friends. She was beautiful, charming, and she made me laugh. She asked me out to dinner the following night and I said yes—that was the beginning of our relationship. We dated for a couple of years before we decided to get a place together. We

Circumstance
Kate Charlton

finally bought our apartment in London. Life was amazing for the first eight years. We both climbed the career ladder, earned decent money, and had the kind of life that a lot of people could only dream of." The memories played in her mind as she described each moment and she only paused long enough to take a deep breath. "Our love life was always good, considering the fact we both worked long hours and we'd been together for so long. I certainly didn't detect a change in her or think that anything was out of the ordinary." She played idly with Helen's lighter, trying to calm her nerves.

Helen sat with her elbow on the table, holding a piña colada in one hand.

"About four years ago, this whole mess started. I'd just finished work and my phone bleeped with a text message that said 'I'm watching you.' I thought it must have been a prank or a wrong number. The following morning, I woke up to two more text messages. 'I know who you are, bitch', and then the other one told me that I'd better start looking over my shoulder."

Helen leaned across the table and pulled Kathy's hand into hers. The look of concern in her eyes was comforting. Relief rushed through her.

"The text messages continued. Anna thought it was most likely a disgruntled former client. Considering the fact that I had no enemies that I was aware of, I thought she was probably right. Changing my number was out of the question because of work, but I kept all the messages and reported it to the police. It's a bit of a big deal when a solicitor is harassing you. Unfortunately, this person wasn't stupid, and the numbers were untraceable: over-the-counter SIM cards put into a ten-quid phone." Kathy rubbed her temples. "And so it went on. I'd get anywhere between one and fifteen text messages a day. Some were threatening, some were creepy, some told me in graphic detail what this person was going to do to me when they decided to 'end the game', as they put it. My car was vandalised three times in one year. Tyres slashed, paint work keyed... It didn't matter that I eventually changed my car. They soon figured it out and started on that one, too. And all the while, Anna insisted that it must be a disgruntled client. She got mad at the police, endlessly frustrated that they didn't seem able to catch this psycho. It got to the point that I thought I was going crazy." She took a long gulp from her glass and pointed at Helen's cigarillos. "Can I have one of those?"

Helen's eyebrow raised. "Are you sure?"

"Yeah."

Circumstance
Kate Charlton

Helen took one from the box and lit it. Kathy rolled the smoke around her mouth and let it out with contentment.

"How long since you quit smoking?" Helen asked with a chuckle.

"Twelve months."

"You don't have to keep going if you don't want to, Kathy."

"I want to. It's surprisingly cathartic. I just hope you don't bolt by the end of the tale."

"I'm not going anywhere," Helen reassured her. Kathy took a moment to collect her thoughts, and then continued.

"So, this madness was now my life. The police were digging into all my old cases and drawing a blank each time. I was alone and scared. Anna was away on business, and I came home one day to find the words 'slut bitch' spray-painted on my front door. Bear in mind that I lived in an apartment with desk security! The security tapes were useless; whoever it was wore a hood and spray painted the cameras out! The security guard was also conveniently away from his desk at the time. On and on it went. Poison pen letters threatening to rape and kill me, damage to my property, constant barrages of text messages that turned into a normal part of my day. This went on for three years, and then the next biggie came." She paused, taking another long drag from the cigarillo. "I'd finished in court shortly after lunchtime and it was a nice day out, so I decided to walk back to the office and pick up something to eat on the way. I cut through the park for the scenery and was about three quarters of the way through when I was rushed from behind and knocked to the ground. I remember the person leaning over me, getting right in my face, and I heard a woman's voice say, 'Get ready, bitch. I'll stab you next time'. I couldn't identify her. I was concussed and she had a hood on and a scarf over her face. I ended up hospitalised overnight. All of this was finally starting to take a toll on my relationship. I was pushing everyone away, including Anna, because I just didn't know who I could trust anymore. I was a nervous wreck, medicated up to the hilt for depression and anxiety."

Helen squeezed Kathy's hand but said nothing.

"The last year of our relationship there was no romance left. Sex was certainly the last thing on my mind. One day I was driving home from work, and for the first time in a long time, I felt quite positive about things. The stalking seemed to have calmed down and there were days when I didn't get a single text message. I thought the nightmare had finally come to an end. I'd stopped taking

Circumstance
Kate Charlton

the diazepam and I was being weaned off the citalopram, too. Anyway, I was driving home through London and stopped at a set of lights on a T-junction. Waited for the lights to go green. Out of nowhere, a car ran the red light to my right and ploughed straight into me, pushing me about a hundred yards down the road before we both stopped. All I remember was the screech of metal, sharp pain in my right side, and the air being knocked out of me by the steering wheel before I passed out."

Helen's frowned.

"It took the fire crew an hour to cut me out of the car. I swear to God my mother must have been looking after me that day, because my only injuries were a couple of busted ribs, a good case of whiplash, and some decent scrapes. The driver of the other car wasn't so lucky and suffered a fractured skull and a ruptured spleen. The police visited me at home a couple of days later and informed me that they'd found a hand-written letter in the glove box of this other car. It was a suicide note. I remember Anna sitting next to me on the sofa, holding my hand, playing the doting girlfriend when the police asked me if I knew who Petra Smythe was. Of course, I'd never heard of the woman, and Anna gave no indication that she had, either. They couldn't go into detail until they could speak to the woman, but they did tell me that this suicide note had mentioned my name. The crash was apparently deliberate. It looked like they'd found my stalker, but I still had no clue who this woman was or why she'd targeted me for so long."

Kathy fell silent for a few moments before delivering the coup de grace of her long and winding tale. "To make a long story short, a couple of weeks later, the police visited again. They arrested Petra Smythe and charged her with dangerous driving, attempted murder, and stalking. Her suicide letter had been quite informative by all accounts. In it, she detailed an affair with Anna. Apparently, when Anna called it off, the woman's mind must have fractured and I was to blame." Kathy inhaled a ragged breath and tried to smile.

"What happened after that?"

"Once the police left, I sat there numb, trying to take everything in. Not only had my partner of twelve years cheated on me, she also sat back for four fucking years and watched this woman torment me and make my life hell. At first, I didn't know what to do. By the time she walked in the door, I was drunk. I said a lot of horrid things to her and rightly so—she just stood there and took it all, apologising repeatedly. She begged me to let her make it up to me, promising we could get through it. I said nothing. All I could think of were the years she allowed that woman to torment me. I was done, and as soon as she went to work the next day, I packed everything I owned and went to my friends Michael and Paul's house to stay until I could get on my feet." She paused long enough to take a swig of her drink. "So, now you know the whole, sordid tale. I'm a middle-aged, essentially homeless lesbian who's been betrayed in a way I never thought possible."

Helen clenched her jaw.

"Say something," Kathy prompted gently.

"I don't even know where to start. I want to kill them both and never let you out of my sight, so they can't hurt you ever again."

Kathy moved her chair closer so she could cuddle into her. "You're my chivalrous doc. I feel very safe when I'm with you. Might sound a bit mad after a week, but life is strange. I've learned that."

"So where is this crazy woman now? And your ex?"

Kathy stroked Helen's thigh, reassured by her presence. "My ex is still in the apartment, though she did try to track me down at Michael and Paul's last week. She was given her marching orders. She kept begging me to take her back. The stalker, last time I heard, was hospitalised and needed multiple surgeries on her leg.

She's now in a secure facility where she's under lock and key."

"And what about you?"

Kathy gave a small shrug. "Rebuilding my life. Moving on. Healing. Helen, take me to bed?"

Without a word, Helen took her by the hand.

Circumstance
Kate Charlton

Chapter 8

Kathy leaned on the balcony, craning her neck so she could take in as much of the ocean before her as possible. The incandescent sun was already blinding on the shimmering surface despite the time of day. It was a mesmerising sight she never tired of. The white tile floor was wonderfully cold underfoot. The only cool part of the island, it seemed. *I'll complain when I get home and it's freezing cold*, she mused.

She'd slept better last night than she'd had for the past five-and-a-half years. Telling Helen everything had been the best thing she'd done in a long time. Her only concern was how Helen took the news and how she'd now view her. She'd spent too long fighting the victim label and she wasn't about to let that change now.

Two strong forearms snaked around her waist and a warm cheek pressed against her ear. "Good morning," Helen greeted, her voice still thick with sleep.

"Good morning to you, too. I feel like I've won the lottery without even buying a ticket," she drawled. Standing in Helen's arms felt like coming home after years in the wilderness.

Circumstance
Kate Charlton

"Well, if you have, I want half and a 1962 Fender bass with six strings."

Kathy had no worldly idea what she was talking about. "In English, Doc!"

"Ah, come on! It's one of the rarest bass guitars in the world! Beautiful, six strings, sunburst design. Playing that baby would sound like God singing!" Her voice rose with excitement. She sounded like a ten-year-old telling Santa what she wanted for Christmas.

Kathy turned around into Helen's embrace and gasped, a smile lighting up her face. "You're stark bollock naked, and people can see you from down there!"

Helen shrugged casually.

"Oh, well. They don't know me," she teased and raised her eyebrows.

Kathy laughed and wrapped her arms around her lover's neck. "Where have you been all my life?"

***

Later that afternoon, they sat on the edge of the pool, the cool water splashing on their legs.

The temperature had soared above a hundred degrees with no breeze to help make the heat bearable. Kathy never complained; it was far better than the cold, dreary days in England.

"Has anyone ever said you look a little bit Glenn Close?" Kathy asked.

Helen smirked and splashed cold pool water over her lover's chest. That earned her a smack on the arm. "Once or fifty times. It's the nose and cheekbones, apparently, though I can't see it myself." She flicked her short locks in a faux-Hollywood celebrity pose.

Kathy laughed.

"Very funny, Miss Kennedy," she mocked. "Okay, I've got a question for you. If you were stuck on a desert island, which book, album, and movie would you take?" She'd realised that she knew very little about the enigmatic woman who was slowly laying claim to her heart. The logical part of her brain told her that she should be terrified by that, but her heart screamed at her to just go with it.

Helen raised her brow and slid off the side and into the pool, and, in one swift movement, she grabbed Kathy by the waist. She fell into the water.

Kathy screamed at the sudden cold, convinced for a moment that she was going to have a heart attack.

Circumstance
Kate Charlton

"Jesus, I only asked a question! No need for such a violent response!" she laughed after finally catching her breath. Her head tingled from the cold that had engulfed her up to her chest.

Helen floated on her back, her skin golden in the sun. "Book would be *Lord of the Flies* by William Goulding. Album is really hard because I love music. Can I take an MP3 player loaded with lots?"

Kathy knitted her brow in a faux attempt to look vexed. "No! That's cheating. Which album could you not live without?"

Helen agonised, as she thought long and hard. "Okay, it would probably have to be Fleetwood Mac's *Rumours*."

"Good choice! I loved them when I was growing up." Kathy agreed. "And movie?"

"Since when did you get all American?" Helen righted herself in the water and pulled Kathy to her. "I think it would have to be *The Graduate*. I was captivated when I first saw it. I must have been about fifteen at the time and I fell head-over-heels in love with Anne Bancroft! Your turn. What are your choices?"

Kathy brushed Helen's damp fringe away from her forehead as she thought about her answers. "Book would probably be *Jane Eyre*. It was so ahead of its time and is an absolute classic. I guess I'm a bit of a geek when it comes to classic books. Movie must be *Breakfast at Tiffany's*, though I think *Bound* would come a close second. Gina Gershon in those muscle shirts, my, my, my!" she giggled cheekily. "My album would have to be Joni Mitchell's *Blue*. My first girlfriend had a copy when I was at university and we'd listen to it repeatedly. "A Case of You" is still my favourite song." She'd spent many evenings lying on her narrow dorm bed, smoking cheap cigarettes and listening to the album. They'd considered themselves so sophisticated at the time, but looking back now, she laughed. They were just girls who knew nothing about the real world.

Helen pulled herself out onto the side of the pool and flicked the water out of her hair as Kathy came to rest between her thighs. "How many girlfriends have you had?"

Kathy's cheeks flushed with heat. "Only three. The first two were short-lived. And then Anna came along. You know how that ended! How about you?"

Helen cleared her throat. "Two serious relationships, including Meg. I dated a few women in between but they were more a case of companionship and good sex. The perks of being young!" she replied, waggling her eyebrows comically.

Circumstance
Kate Charlton

"Oh, so you were a lothario in your youth."

Helen gave a cheeky wink. "Well, I never had any complaints."

Kathy laughed and pulled Helen's long legs down into the cold pool. The scream it elicited could have roused an entire island. Instantly, she turned and pulled Kathy under with her. In the depth of the water, they held onto one another until their lungs begged for air.

***

Helen ran her fingertips over the rough surface of the table in her room, her brow creased in deep thought. She watched as the sun disappeared beneath the horizon and sighed. Soon, their lives would change. Her flight home was in two days. That meant only two more nights with Kathy. It made her feel empty inside, to the point of nausea.

"When do you have to go back to work?" she asked Kathy without looking up.

"Next Monday. It gives me a little time to get my laundry and everything else done when I get back." Her tone was as flat as Helen's.

"Would you consider coming up to stay with me in Newcastle when you get back? Maybe until Sunday evening?" Her eyes rolled up slowly, afraid that she'd see Kathy laughing at the idea.

Kathy's face softened. "My flight lands early evening on Thursday. An hour or so to get home from the airport, an hour to pack a bag…. I can probably be in Newcastle by eleven or so that night."

"Is that a yes?"

Kathy giggled and reached for her hand across the table. "Of course it's a yes, but I'll have to leave early Sunday morning. I've got things I really need to do before I go back to work and I need to find a flat before I overstay my welcome."

Helen fiddled with the signet ring on her right pinkie and gave a half nod. "We have lawyers in Newcastle, you know. And places to live. Cheaper than London, too."

Kathy nudged with her foot. "Hold your horses, Doc. You still don't know me that well; I might drive you crazy back in the real world."

"I doubt that very much."

***

The next two days were a battle to remain upbeat and cheerful; both women had post-holiday blues to contend with along with the knowledge that things would be very different for them in their everyday lives. Sure, it was only five hours in the car or four on the train, but it wasn't as though they would be able to see each other every day, despite the wonders of modern technology and video calls.

On Wednesday afternoon, the atmosphere was like that of a wake. They'd cried in each other's arms, made love for the last time on their paradise island, and sat together on the front steps of the hotel, waiting for the bus to take Helen to the airport.

"I'll see you tomorrow night, yes?" Helen asked.

"And I'll message you the minute I get home."

"I'll be waiting. Safe journey."

"Helen?" Kathy cupped her face in her hands. "I love you."

Helen sniffed, trying to stop the tears from falling. "I love you, too."

They walked to the foot of the coach steps, neither of them wanting to let go of the other's hand. As she climbed the first step, Helen kissed Kathy's palm for the last time before pulling herself away and onto the bus. In that moment, she felt so empty and lost. She knew it was crazy. They'd be reunited the following evening, but her heart still ached.

***

Althaia pulled out a chair without waiting to be asked and sat next to Kathy. She rested her elbows on the table, perching on the edge of the seat as she regarded Kathy in front of her. "She's gone home, yes?"

Kathy lit a cigarette. She knew that smoking again was stupid, but she needed something to calm herself. She promised herself she'd give them up when she got home. "This afternoon, yes. It's feels like a very long day today and I'm finding it hard being here without her."

"She loves you, you know? I've watched her, the way she looks at you when she thinks you won't notice. Her whole face changes when you're in her sights. I can't really explain it, but she looks so much softer."

"You think so?"

"I know so," Althaia said. "I've always been sweet on Helen. Always a pleasure to see her when she comes here but always with a beautiful woman on her arm, yes? Her wife, now you."

Circumstance
Kate Charlton

Kathy studied the younger woman's features and realised for the first time just how beautiful she truly was. "Why don't you have a girlfriend, Althaia?"

Althaia grinned, showing her perfect white teeth.

"I have a dog, and that's enough!" she joked. "I work long and hard hours, sometimes more than twelve a day, seven days a week. This country, this place, it's not always easy to find like-minded people, you know what I mean? Most of the gay women I meet are here on holiday and most of them are here with their girlfriend. What's a girl to do?" She gave a tiny shrug but there was sadness behind her words.

It occurred to Kathy how lucky she was. Being gay and British was no big deal anymore. "You'll find the right woman eventually."

"Yes. Don't let her go, my friend. She loves you." With that, Althaia stood abruptly and returned to work.

***

Helen hated to fly. She disliked it even more today. The queues in the airport had been crazy and it felt like they were treating the passengers like cattle. Even though she was grateful the flight took off on time, sadness pulled at her heart the as the distance between her and Kathy grew.

Circumstance
Kate Charlton

Well into the flight, a stewardess who was taking drink orders stopped and looked down at Helen. "Is there anything I can get for you?"

Helen half-smiled. "A whisky on the rocks will do." What she wanted was Kathy in the seat next to her. She checked her watch. *Ten o'clock. She'll be watching the entertainment or reading in her room. I wonder if she's missing me as much as I'm missing her right now.* Overanalysing everything had always been one of her quirks; it never did her any good. She loved how Kathy made her feel about life and about herself. She'd felt more like her old self since she'd met Kathy than she had in the past year and a half. She loved how well their bodies fit together and how smiling became so easy again. She closed her eyes and let her mind wander back to the Greek island where she'd left her heart.

Circumstance
Kate Charlton

Circumstance
Kate Charlton

Chapter 9

The room began to close in on Petra, making it hard for her to pace between a narrow bed with a wafer-thin mattress and a built-in wardrobe without doors. She lay on her back on the sad excuse of the bed, her arms behind her head to give a little more comfort than the cheap pillow allowed, and stared at the ceiling. Patterns and shapes appeared. Her original idea may not have been her brightest, but she wouldn't let herself down again.

It infuriated her how Anna let her sit and rot, and then Kathy's face flashed in her mind and her anger built. *It's her fault I'm in here, and she's gonna pay for it.*

Thoughts raced through her head. Anna had been the person who had walked into her life and helped her turn into the person she was meant to be, the person who learned to love so completely and embrace life again. That wasn't something she was ever prepared to lose. She closed her eyes and allowed her imagination to wander, to make plans that would let her reclaim her life.

***

After months of being sedated and held in a tiny room, she'd finally been given permission to walk around the courtyard. She took several deep breaths, then sighed

Circumstance
Kate Charlton

when she gazed at her surroundings. In every direction, chain-link fence with barbed wire attached to the top reminded her where she was and why she was there. If only she was allowed to go out the front door… But the only patients who ventured past the double doors were those who were nearing release. Petra had no idea if and when she would be allowed to leave, and she had no intention of waiting for the courts to determine her fate.

"Move it, Smythe," the guard yelled.

She walked the perimeter of the courtyard three times before she was directed inside.

At breakfast, she sat on a hard-plastic chair at the Formica table and looked around at the saps in the hall as they sucked down eggs that looked like rubber, accompanied by greasy, undercooked bacon. They all seemed happy to be there—not that she got close enough to any of them to find out for sure. She was way above them in class, education, and lifestyle, and observed them all in silence, her finger rubbing over her rough thumbnail until it became sore.

Everything was beige—the walls, the flooring. No wonder people went crazy.

Circumstance
Kate Charlton

The more she looked around at the crazed faces, the more her heart felt like it was about to explode in her chest.

"I need to make a call," she told one of the male staff members. He scowled at her.

"*I need, I need.* I'm so bloody tired of what you need. You'll get what we give you." He turned on his heels and stormed off.

"You piece of shit," she grumbled.

***

She sat in the corner of the claustrophobic room, her eyes red from tears, and rested her forehead on her knees as she tried to breathe deeply, but nothing worked. Exhaustion had both physically and mentally attacked her. *All I wanted was a phone call. One fucking phone call!* She needed to hear Anna's voice. *I'll be out of this dump in two clicks of my fingers.* Time was on her side. Once they let her out of her cell, she would act like the subservient patient, and when the guards became distracted by the fight she'd already planned on creating between the two alpha males, she'd walk out and no one would notice.

***

Circumstance
Kate Charlton

In the crowded sitting room, Petra stepped back as the two patients began to fight. Hospital staff rushed in and tried to pull them apart. The one lone nurse who directed the other patients to move away did not notice as Petra slid past her. Once outside the double doors, she took off running and managed to scale the fence with a strength and agility she'd forgotten she had. Years of gym work and core fitness classes had paid off. She couldn't believe she'd managed to do it—the plan worked better than she'd imagined.

The wooded area around the psychiatric facility offered her enough coverage that she wouldn't be seen from overhead. She didn't realize how far she'd gotten until day broke and the busy London highway came into view.

In her heart, she knew that Anna would be waiting for her, but she was going to have to lie low for a while so they wouldn't catch her and send her back to that godawful place. She understood why Anna had had to lie about her and their love. It was a protection mechanism for both of them against that bitch. Kathy was the only thing that stood in their way. The fact that Petra hadn't been killed in the car crash was a sign that she and Anna were meant for one another. She just had to make sure she did things properly this time.

Chapter 10

"Hey, toots! Did you miss me, or did your holiday romance wipe all thoughts of little old me from your mind?" Michael asked as he plonked Kathy down. He took charge of her suitcase and directed her to the airport exit.

A smile stretched her lips. "I always miss you."

"Like a hole in the head, I bet. And do we have any holiday pics to look at? I'd like to know who's stolen the heart of my BFF."

"Maybe." *I'm always asking him for help, but I don't have too many friends to rely on.* "Michael, I hate to ask another favour from you, but how quickly can you get me home and then to Kings Cross station? I'm heading to Newcastle."

Michael winked at her.

"Then I guess we'd better hurry."

They stopped outside the main doors. A gust of cold wind whipped around them. The sky had darkened to gravel-grey, and people were running for cover. A surprise rainstorm with heavy drops drumming over the pavement with force had caught everyone out.

"We're going to have to make a mad dash to the car," Michael said, pulling the collar of his jacket up around his neck.

Looking down at her feet, Kathy let out a soft sigh of defeat. "Crap! These sandals are going to be ruined."

"Women!" Michael joked.

***

A brilliant flash of lightning ripped through the city skyline, then three seconds later a boom of thunder cracked directly over the car as they merged onto the motorway. The heavy rain then turned into an avalanche of ice pellets bouncing on car windshields like ping pong balls. The traffic slowed, with a few drivers having to hit their brakes hard while others veered sideways over the slippery white surface.

"Jesus, why can't people learn to drive? I can probably get you home in forty-five minutes, but if this storm keeps up, it might take a bit longer. Why are you going to Newcastle?"

"That's where Helen lives."

Circumstance
Kate Charlton

"But you've only just left her. That's the fucking trouble with lesbians, they keep U-Haul in business."

"That really pisses me off. No, we don't all fall in love and move in together the next day."

"A little touchy, aren't we?"

"No. I'm just tired, and I know what I want, and I know Helen feels the same."

"So, come on, spill. Rhodes is fabulous, but I want to know all about this woman you're shooting off to see."

Lightness filled her chest.

"I really like her, Michael. She excites and scares me at the same time. I don't mean scare in a negative way, more like…she makes me feel alive, and I haven't felt like that for years. She's beautiful in every way possible. I know how crazy I sound, but I believe she's the one for me."

Michael nodded in consideration. "You might just be right. Everyone said that Paul and I wouldn't last, but look at us now. What are you going to do about Anna?"

Kathy swallowed hard and shrugged. "I'm not going to do anything. She and I are through. I'm planning on house hunting because there are too many memories in that apartment. I don't want to live there anymore. A fresh start will do me good, don't you think? We weren't married, and I'm so glad about that."

"I can't see her giving you up so easily," Michael said. "She's not the type. You know what her ego's like."

"Michael, she doesn't get a say in this. She blew everything out of the water when she started sleeping with that awful woman. I just want her out of my life. For good."

***

Helen had been to the grocery store to stock up on fresh fruits and veggies and a few luxurious items she thought Kathy might like. She couldn't stop grinning like a teenager in love, and she hummed different melodies while she cleaned the house from top to bottom even though it was already immaculate. *Meg, I know this is our home, and I'll treasure that forever. Please be happy for me, my darling. But I think it's time for me to move forward. I love the memories we shared in this house. No one will ever be able to replace those. And I'm sure you'd have loved Kathy if the two of you had met in life...*

***

The Central Station platform was light and airy with its glass-panelled domed roof, but even though the sunlight was warm through the glass, the wind became a challenge inside the tunnel-shaped architecture.

The sound of the train in the distance brought Helen back. She looked on and, for the first time since she'd met Kathy, insecurity formed a knot in her stomach. The irrational side of her brain worried that Kathy wouldn't be on it. *When did I start to second-guess everything?*

An announcement over the speakers informed travellers the next train to stop was Kings Cross to Newcastle. A cold wind whipped through the station just as the train glided up to the platform. The enormous coupled carriages blocked the daylight as they passed before drawing to a halt. Doors opened, and crowds of people boarded while others departed, creating a confusing jumble of bodies. Helen stood on tip-toe to see if she could locate Kathy in the mass of oncoming travellers. *Where are you?*

The conductor walked alongside the cars, shutting each door with a slam as he made his way to the locomotive. When the last door had been closed, he blew his whistle and a noisy hiss came from the airbrakes. Then, as dramatically as it had entered the station, the train moved—a few small jerks signifying its departure.

"Fuck, she didn't come. I should've known. Oh, what a fool I've been, to think someone would want…"

Circumstance
Kate Charlton

"Helen?" a timid voice asked. "Are you talking to yourself?"

Helen placed her hand over her chest and whirled around to greet her lover. Overwhelmed with joyful tears, she held her arms out and embraced Kathy with a heartfelt hug. "I didn't think you'd come."

"How could I not?"

***

The nineteenth-century cottage amazed Kathy when it came into view at the end of the drive. It oozed character with its overhanging eaves, dormer windows, and red-tiled roof. *Oh, this is very Helen.* Once inside, she let herself be led into a spotless kitchen with a huge island and all the mod cons a professional chef could ever dream of.

"You're a cordon bleu chef, too?" she teased.

"No, Meg was the cook. She had it all redesigned when we bought this place. I get by in the kitchen, but it isn't a whole load of fun cooking for one." She pulled a bottle of red wine from a rustic wooden rack on the countertop. "Do you like Bordeaux?"

"I do."

Circumstance
Kate Charlton

"You have good taste in wine." Helen opened the bottle with a corkscrew, then slowly poured the red liquid into two large glass goblets. The fruity bouquet filled the air when she picked up the glasses and handed one to Kathy.

Their fingers brushed in a light touch and Kathy immediately acted on it by pulling Helen in close. She looked into her eyes, and, drawn by her desirous gaze, moved in for a hello kiss. Their mouths opened, and softly they pressed their lips together. She lost track of time as Helen's tongue caressed hers.

As they pulled out of the kiss, Kathy brushed a strand of hair away from Helen's eyes, then took a sip of her wine.

"Mmm, it's velvety," she said. "Now, I'm getting a secondary taste. Notes of tobacco, and leather, and some earthy flavours."

"Well, this vintage has been in the bottle for ten years. I consider it to still be on the younger side, but it does have a unique character, just like you."

***

The shrill ringing of her mobile phone dragged Kathy out of a deep sleep, and she grappled for the device.

Circumstance
Kate Charlton

"Yeah?" she asked, still not fully awake.

Helen turned over beside her and threw an arm over Kathy in her sleep.

"Is that you, Kath? It's Michael."

"Michael? What the hell time is it?" she asked, propping herself up onto one elbow.

"It's shortly after four, sweetie. Look, Kathy, are you somewhere safe?" he asked. His voice was tense, and his usual jovial tone gone.

"Of course I am. I'm at Helen's place. What's going on, Michael?" She knew whatever it was, it couldn't be good for him to be calling her in the middle of the night. "Has something happened to Paul?"

"No, sweetie. Paul's fine."

Helen stirred beside her and propped her chin on Kathy's shoulder.

"The police were here about half an hour ago. Petra Smythe has escaped."

"Escaped? What the hell do you mean *escaped*? She's not bloody Houdini, Michael!"

"She managed to do a bunk when she was on grounds leave at the psychiatric facility yesterday evening. The

police haven't been able to locate her. She's seemingly dropped off the face of the earth. They came here to tell you tonight."

Kathy pinched the bridge of her nose as the beginnings of a headache pounded at her temples.

"Are you there, Kath?" he asked.

"I'm here," she responded.

"No one knows where you are apart from Paul and I, so you're safe there. The entire Met are out looking for her, so they'll have her in no time. I just thought you should know."

Kathy's lips were numb.

"Keep me posted." Her mind reeled. Her stalker was on the loose and there was no telling what damage she could do.

"What's going on, Kathy?" Helen asked.

"Tea. I need…no, I need a stiff drink."

***

They sat at the kitchen island, illuminated by worktop low lights. After the news they'd received, it was unlikely either of them would get back to sleep any time soon. Coffee seemed to be the only answer.

"I wouldn't blame you if you wanted to put me on the first train back to London. You don't need all of this drama, Helen."

"Enough. I won't hear talk like that. I'm in this for the long haul. It takes more than a crazy woman to put me off, and Michael's probably right. They'll have her banged up again by this time tomorrow, you'll see." She took two cigarettes from Kathy's pack and lit one for each of them.

Kathy took it gratefully. "So much for quitting again after my holiday."

"I'll make a deal with you. Once they catch her, I'll quit with you," Helen countered.

Kathy tried to smile, but her stomach churned. The police hadn't been able to catch Petra Smythe before. What if they couldn't catch her now?

Circumstance
Kate Charlton

Chapter 11

The next day passed in a blur. Kathy tried to lose herself in Helen's presence, but it was impossible. She kept picturing Petra's face looming over hers.

That evening, listening to the sound of rain tapping against the window pane, an owl hooting in the distance, and Helen's soft breathing next to her, Kathy soon drifted off into a deep sleep.

At some point during the night, that sleep became erratic. Her body temperature climbed to the point where she overheated and kicked off the bed covers, then flailed her arms and caught Helen's face with her hand.

Helen immediately woke and pushed the hand from her face, then sat up and turned on the night lamp next to her.

"Honey. Honey, wake up," she called as she rocked Kathy gently. "God, you're sweating like crazy!"

Kathy screamed out. Her eyes flashed open and burst into tears.

"What is it? What's wrong?"

Circumstance
Kate Charlton

Breathing wildly and blinking fast, Kathy took a few moments to gather her thoughts and bring herself back to the present. "I keep having the same goddamn nightmare. It just won't go away. It's so vivid, like I'm really there. I can see everything, feel everything. It scares me so much."

"What's the nightmare about?"

Tears fell from her eyes and dispersed onto the sheets. "It starts with the sound of metal screeching, then I taste blood, and I can't scream. I'm in pain, a lot of pain, and I'm inside a crumpled car with the airbag crushing my lungs." She pulled away, needing to put space between her and Helen.

***

The sound of her grumbling stomach reminded Helen it was lunchtime.

"I'm famished." She moved around the kitchen. "How about lunch?"

The front door burst open, bringing in a draught of cool air followed by the sound of a small army filling the house. A boy and a girl came skidding into the kitchen, followed by a lumbering golden retriever who was just as excited. Shouts of "calm down, kids" came from a male voice in the hallway as the two children threw themselves at Helen, who scooped them up in her arms.

"Oh no, it's the terrible twins!" she shouted with glee.

A man stood in the doorway while the carnage died down.

"Hi, sis. Sorry, I didn't know you had company!"

Helen lowered the screaming children and grinned broadly.

"Kathy, this bear of a man is David, my brother, and these two little weasels are Hannah and Thomas, my niece and nephew. Your new friend there is Barney, the most well-behaved member of the clan."

David crossed the kitchen with surprising agility—his shorts-clad legs looked like he could easily contend in a World's Strongest Man contest. Kathy held out her hand and accepted his warm greeting.

"Aunty Helen, is this your new girlfriend?" Hannah asked.

Kathy felt the heat rising from the base of her throat to the roots of her hair.

"Yes, Hannah, this is Kathy and she's my girlfriend."

Circumstance
Kate Charlton

David's caterpillar eyebrows rose up to his hairline. "Kept that one quiet, sister of mine!" He kissed her cheek and crossed to the kettle to make coffee. "The kids were excited to see you, probably because the little mercenaries want to know what you've bought them. I'm more interested in this beautiful lady who's crazy enough to find you attractive."

"I'm Kathy, forty-two, solicitor, and your darling sister has swept me off my feet." Her smile was genuine. The hubbub was enough to make her forget her situation, at least for a little while.

"And considerably well-spoken. You can't be from around here?"

"No, I'm a London girl," she answered.

"Solicitor, eh? Criminal law?" he continued to probe.

"Intellectual property law. In my case, the world of the printed word. Not quite as glamourous."

"David's a detective. I do apologise for his grilling!" Helen interrupted, jumping up from her stool to fetch the children's gifts from the living room. "Where's Andrea?"

"She's at work today, so I'm on daddy-duty with the terrible twins."

Circumstance
Kate Charlton

"Ah, I see. So you thought you'd come and see big sister to help you out and take the pressure off, eh?" She knew her younger brother so well.

"Daddy said that if we told you we loved you enough, you'd come with us to the Discovery place and show us cool stuff," Thomas chimed in from the floor, intent on ripping open the paper that covered his gift.

Helen narrowed her eyes at her brother, who held up his hands in mock surrender. "Did he now?" She turned her attention to her lover. "What do you think, darling? Can you cope with a day out with this lot?"

Kathy pretended to consider the idea for a moment. "I think I'd like you to show me some cool stuff, too."

***

Petra had managed to get herself sorted out: money in her pocket and a room in a non-descript bed and breakfast. Even though it wasn't home, it beat the psychiatric facility hands down. What pleased her most and eased her mind was the fact that she'd been able to get a phone. It was cheap, but it suited her purposes and gave her a connection to the real world.

It irritated her that she couldn't get hold of Anna, but she understood how careful they had to be and why her soulmate found it difficult to reply to her. *That fucking bitch Kathy!* The white heat of anger had been the one thing keeping her going.

She needed to put an end to this. Her and Anna's happiness relied upon it. She'd promised Anna after they first met that she would take care of her, and that was a promise she did not plan on breaking.

***

Kathy was engrossed in a display of a World War II soldier's uniform when her phone vibrated in her jeans pocket. She pulled it out absentmindedly, expecting a text from Michael, but she didn't recognise the number. The message said: *They won't find me, but I'll make sure I find you.* A sick sensation swirled in her stomach as the phone slipped from her grip and skittered across the wooden floor.

Helen rushed to her side and placed her hands around her shoulders. "What is it?"

"Petra."

Helen picked the phone up from the floor and swiped the screen to read the message, with David reading it over her shoulder at the same time.

"What the fuck?" he asked quietly.

Circumstance
Kate Charlton

"Kathy's had issues with a stalker who's done a runner from the secure hospital she'd been placed in," Helen informed him.

"Do the police know about this?" he asked, looking at Kathy.

"Oh, yeah. They know all about it. This is the first time she's contacted me since she was arrested, though. Clearly the psychiatric treatment hasn't done any good!" Her voice waivered as she thought about the potential consequences. *She could be watching me right now and I wouldn't have a clue. What if she is? What if she's planned out her next move already and I'm just a sitting duck?* The hairs on the nape of her neck stiffened, her palms turned clammy, and her stomach threatened to revolt.

***

Once back in the safety of the house, Kathy rested comfortably on the sofa as Helen expertly massaged her feet. The text message had ripped through her like a jagged knife through flesh. Even though she'd reported it to her local police station, she had a feeling it was only going to get worse.

"Why don't you stay here? Until they have her back in the hospital, at least," Helen asked.

Circumstance
Kate Charlton

"Honey, there's nothing I'd love more, but I can't. I can't afford to lose my job as well as everything else. It's a dog-eat-dog world, and no matter how long I've been employed there, they'll replace me in a heartbeat if I keep taking time off."

Helen clenched her toes through the plush cream carpet. "I'm worried for you. She knows where you work, and it won't be hard for her to find out where you're staying…"

Kathy brought a finger to Helen's lips. "Helen, I've lived with this for so long, I can't remember what life was like before it all started. I know what you're saying, and you've showed me more kindness and compassion in the past couple of weeks than Anna did in all our years together."

"That's because she's a…" Helen tried to mumble around the finger covering her lips.

"I can't keep running away for the rest of my life, and I don't know when, or if, this will ever end, but I do know I have to stand up and fight. I'm returning to London with my head held high and finding myself a place to rent. I don't want to tie myself down by buying anywhere yet, but it's a start."

Chapter 12

The next two weeks flew by for Kathy. She'd found a new apartment within days of returning to London, thanks to an old work colleague, and was now preparing to move in. She'd had several emails and phone calls from Anna, begging her for a second chance and pathetically apologising. She wondered how it had taken her so long to see through the woman she'd spent so many years of her life loving. Anna was no longer the same woman—any feelings she'd once had were now gone. The only things she felt for her now were resentment and anger.

Though the rent was suitably London-exorbitant, and the location perfect, the apartment was quite small.

Helen, red-faced and wheezing, lumbered into the lounge carrying a large box.

"What the hell's in this thing?" she groaned, dropping it in the middle of the living room floor with a resounding thud.

Kathy let out a hearty laugh as she kissed Helen. "That would be legal reference books!"

An expletive-laden rant came from the front door as Michael and Paul fought to get a king-sized mattress through it. Helen and Kathy rushed to assist but were no help when they were unable to control their laughter at the sight of Paul completely trapped between the mattress and doorframe.

A tall, flame-haired woman casually sauntered in behind them after the mattress was finally wrestled through the narrow doorway. She was the only one who wasn't suitably dressed for moving boxes and furniture.

"I will gladly unpack your new kitchen equipment, sweetie, but I swear, if I break a nail, I'm suing you!" she exclaimed.

"Emma, you're such a drama queen, but you know I love you for this." Kathy pecked her on the cheek—as different as they were, the two of them had forged a close friendship in the nine years that they'd worked together.

Helen shook her head as the redhead sashayed into the kitchen, arms loaded with John Lewis bags brimming with gadgets that would fit on the small countertop.

Kathy cupped her hand on Helen's chin and turned her head to face her. "I'm this way, sweetie. Emma's extremely straight, and I don't share."

Rubbing her hands on her plaid shirt, Helen pulled Kathy into her arms pressed their lips together. "I'm not going anywhere."

Circumstance
Kate Charlton

"Urgh! Lesbians!" Paul broke in with mock disgust. The women pulled away from each other, laughing at his reaction. "I really don't know why we're putting ourselves through all of this. I have a feeling you'll be telling us you're moving to Newcastle within three months—mark my words!" He waved his hand in the air and spun around. "Never mind. Onwards, buttercup! Michael and I are going to put your bed together so that you two humping bunnies can christen it tonight. Not before you take us and Princess Break-a-Nail in there out for dinner, though!"

"I heard that!" came Michael's snooty response from the kitchen.

"You were meant to, darling! I might even have a shave for you tonight!" Paul shouted back in good humour, his hand running over the silver stubble on his chin. "I'm too fucking old for this shit!" He let out a hearty laugh and ambled back to the bedroom.

Kathy knew Paul was probably right, but it wouldn't be three months from now. She needed a little time to stand on her own two feet. It was a liberating feeling, knowing that she was doing this for herself and not for anyone else. It was also humbling to know that Helen was behind her all the way and had supported her every decision. Not to say she didn't protest, but she gave in and bought Kathy a panic alarm and made her promise to carry it with her no matter what when she returned to London.

In the doorway between the kitchen and sitting room, she watched everyone feverishly work to help organize her life. Instantly, she was filled with gratitude for the people in her life, and was reminded in that moment just how lucky she was.

"I'm fading," Michael's voice bellowed from the other side of the door.

"We're almost changed," Kathy called back. She sat on the edge of the bed while Helen tucked the shirttails of her white silk blouse into her black jeans. Dinner was the last thing on her mind; all she could think of was ripping that shirt off of Helen and taking her right there, but then they'd never make it to the restaurant.

Helen smiled over her shoulder and winked. "I know that look. Don't lose it. When we get back tonight, we have to 'hump like bunnies'. His words, not mine."

They both laughed but fell silent when Kathy crossed the room and took Helen in her arms. "Have I told lately how lucky I am?"

"I think that's the other way around."

Circumstance
Kate Charlton

Kathy smiled and smacked Helen o̲n̲ ̲t̲h̲e̲ ̲a̲r̲s̲e̲ ̲a̲s̲ ̲s̲h̲e̲ stepped back so she could finish getting ̲r̲e̲a̲d̲y̲.̲ ̲I̲f̲ someone had told her a year ago that her heart woulḏ ̲b̲e̲ lost to the most gorgeous soft butch she'd ever met, Kathy would've thought them crazy. Yet here she was. She wondered where they would be in ten years' time. She imagined the two of them sitting in Helen's garden, sipping red wine and watching the sun set, going on holidays together, making each other dinner. It should have scared her how easily she could visualise it all, but it didn't.

Helen pulled on her suit jacket and grinned. "You look lost in deep and meaningful thought there, young lady!"

Kathy stood and smoothed down the cocktail dress that hung elegantly from one shoulder.

"Just counting my blessings!" She planted a kiss on Helen's cheek, breathing in the now-familiar scent that transported her straight back to a small Greek island.

***

It hadn't been hard to track Kathy Harland down. The stupid bitch still worked in the same place and parked her car in the same parking space. Sure, it was a different car after the accident, but it was easy enough to wait and watch to see which one she got into at the end of the work ay. Petra had bought herself a cheap car from a newspaper ad she'd found and had no intention of insuring it. It would be like holding up a sign saying 'Here I am!'

She forced herself to sit still in the car the first time she saw Kathy exit the lift. She was the same self-assured, stuck-up bitch Petra remembered. Every fibre of Petra's being throbbed with hatred for the woman who stood between her and Anna, but she knew she had to bide her time.

Each day for the past week, she followed her, sometimes in the car and sometimes on foot, and watched her coming and going from the friends' house she was staying at.

It infuriated her to watch Kathy and her friends unpack a moving truck. It wasn't an unusual setting for someone moving, but the interaction Kathy had with one of the women confused her. Their body language suggested more than just friendship, with little touches here, glances there, and the way they absentmindedly threw their arms around each other. *Surely that bitch can't be cheating on Anna?*

If Anna would pick up her phone, there wouldn't be so many unanswered questions.

Circumstance
Kate Charlton

***

The Chinese restaurant was bustling with patrons enjoying their Saturday night, many already on their way to being merry. Kathy clung to Helen's hand as they were led through a maze of tightly-packed tables decked with red tablecloths and Chinese fans. Michael, Paul, and Emma were already seated, drinks in hand, and trading their traditional barbs with each other. It was a sign of affection.

They had the best seats in the house, right next to the window, where they could watch the world pass them by. Despite their aching muscles, they all looked relaxed.

"Michael, is that another new suit?" Kathy asked as they were seated.

Michael winced, took a sip of his martini, and groaned. "Don't get him started!"

Paul jabbed a finger in his husband's direction. "You see, I told you that you didn't need another suit!"

Kathy had just inadvertently started World War Three.

"I work in fashion editing! A man cannot have too many suits, or clothes for that matter, in my line of work. It's important to be seen keeping up with the trends."

Emma rolled her eyes and feigned a yawn.

"Pipe down, boys! Enough already!" she teased.

The waiter broke into their revelry and took a further round of drink orders. No one felt brave enough to go for sake and they all chose cocktails instead. Spirits were high as the five friends shared jokes and got to know Helen better. She was now as much a feature in their lives as Kathy, and they were all quietly thankful to the GP for putting a smile back on their closest friend's face.

Kathy almost jumped out of her skin as glass smashed against the ground from the table behind her. Before the accident, it wouldn't have bothered her, but now… She glanced over her shoulder. A young waiter was sweeping up a pile of broken dishes. Her nerves continued to jangle as the head waiter berated the poor guy in Chinese. Her friends broke into laughter, and she realized she hadn't been listening. Not wanting to appear rude, she smiled and laughed along.

"That's funny. Tell me more." Emma leaned over the table, hanging on Michael's every word. He loved being the centre of attention at a dinner table and everyone loved to listen to his crazy tales.

"Well, what could I do? He was a rock star and I'd just puked on his shoes! I was twenty-three and as green as grass at interviewing. Besides, it was my first real job. I offered him a blowjob and pretended it never happened!"

His audience laughed uproariously, knowing that Michael would have done exactly what he said. Kathy dabbed at the tears that threatened to spill over her eyelids and ruin her mascara. She hadn't laughed so much in months. As the laughter died down, a dull thud sounded on the window right beside her. She jumped for the second time that night, pressing herself hard against Helen's body. The person outside the window pressed lewdly against the glass, a black hood pulled up over their head.

The dark figure was very female, and her gaze was trained on Kathy alone. The twisted grin on her face was maniacal as she brought her fingers to her lips and wiggled her tongue between them in a lecherous gesture before running her finger across her throat. The smile fell from her lips, contorting her features into a look of pure evil.

Kathy screamed, and the woman took off running down the road. Michael and Paul almost upended the table in their haste to run out of the restaurant after her.

"Oh my God, that was her! That was fucking Petra!" Kathy cried into Helen's shoulder, clinging to her jacket lapel as though she was going to evaporate from her grasp.

The two men came back into the restaurant five minutes later. They'd lost Petra in the crowded London streets. Helen sat with her arm around Kathy's shoulders. Emma pressed her mobile phone to her ear, a finger in the other to block out the hubbub of the restaurant as she spoke to the police dispatcher on the other end.

"Ask them to come to the apartment please, Emma," Kathy whispered. "I don't want to stay here."

***

Kathy sipped on the brandy that Paul had poured, her whole body still shaking. A wonderful night had been reduced to a tainted mess as they all sat waiting for the police to arrive.

Helen's rage bubbled just below the surface, but she fought to keep it under control for her lover's sake. Petra had followed them, and that meant that she must know where Kathy lived. The thought terrified her, and she wondered how she could ever leave her alone.

"I'm going to have someone come and fit extra security equipment tomorrow," Michael announced. "I know you've got security on the door downstairs, but she got past them in your old place, so we're not going to take any chances. You need door alarms on your front door and on your patio doors."

"It's a rented apartment, Michael, I can't just turn the place into Fort Knox."

"Fuck that!" Michael snapped. "If the landlord doesn't like it, you can move back in with us, but this is what we're going to do."

Helen paced the room. She wanted to find the crazy bitch and kick the living crap out of her. She regarded Kathy's puffy face and streaked mascara. If it was the last thing she ever did, she'd make that woman pay.

When the doorbell rang, Kathy sat back and looked to Michael, who was already walking to the door.

"Stay here, I'll get it."

Of course, the police said all the right things, took statements to add to the pile that they already had regarding Petra Smythe, and promised they'd be in touch as soon as they had any new information. No one was under any illusions—London was an enormous rabbit warren of a city and the perfect place to hide in plain sight. Petra was a woman who had worked in an extremely well-paid job and certainly wouldn't have to worry about access to cash. She could hide forever if she really wanted to. Life had to go on.

Circumstance
Kate Charlton

***

In her car, Petra watched the police arrive, then leave, laughing as she recalled the look on that whore's face.

She'd loved that expression, and the way she'd jumped into that butch's arms when she leaned against the glass. *They're obviously screwing each other*. She tightened her blonde ponytail, the elastic band nipping her scalp. As much as she wanted Kathy out of Anna's life, she wouldn't stand back and let Kathy trample all over her.

Chapter 13

A young mother struggled as she pushed a baby in a pram with one hand and dragged a screaming three-year-old with the other. It was a scene that Helen witnessed all too frequently. She saw a lot of deprivation in Newcastle, and it still amazed her after so many years in practice how things would still cause her eyebrows to raise on a regular basis.

Her amethyst drop earrings swayed as she stretched her arms above her head, the crick in her back popping nicely. It was strange that she still thought of herself as eighteen, but her body gave her true age away every day. She meandered into the break room and rummaged through the fridge for her salad, glad it wasn't her turn for home visits. They always resulted in sticky carpeted bungalows, weird substances adhering to her clothes, and at least three care home visits for patients who 'just didn't seem right'. She flopped into a chair and pulled off the Tupperware lid, uninspired by its contents.

Ramesh laughed at her, watching how Helen's lip curled in disgust.

"I don't understand why you eat that shit day in and day out when you pull the same face at it every time. It's not going to magically turn into steak and chips, you know."

Helen scowled at her Indian partner.

"Just because you live on stodge and shite and never get fat!" she retorted petulantly, then stabbed at the lettuce leaf and crammed it into her mouth.

"I go to the gym, that's why! Anyway, if Julie knew what I ate at work, she'd kill me."

"I go to the bloody gym, but I still have to eat well. Age is creeping up on me."

Ramesh laughed heartily, his well-tied turban never moving. She never understood how he managed that.

"You're a grumpy bitch this morning. What's wrong with you?" he asked.

"So far, my day has consisted of ADHD Chesney with an ear infection, Mrs. Crouch with cellulitis, and Mr. Turpin's non-existent piles." Helen paused, twisting the signet ring absent-mindedly around her finger. "You know, I'm sure that man just likes to have me shove my fingers up his arse!" She shuddered at the thought as her Ramesh released a huge belly laugh.

Circumstance
Kate Charlton

"Welcome to my world. I've also seen cellulitis, a chest infection, one post-natal depression, and a common cold that snuck past the reception desk."

"I need another vacation."

"You have two lovely days away from snot and bottoms. What are you doing with them?"

Helen's features brightened. "Well, Kathy's coming to stay for the weekend. She'll leave once she finishes work, but she's unlikely to arrive before midnight. Still, at least she'll be here."

"You're still in the honeymoon period." He smirked, twisting the end of his moustache. "How long has it been now?"

"We've been together for just over three months; our holiday seems so long ago!" she whined.

"And now you have your Christmas to look forward to. Don't be going all Bah Humbug on me; it's only a month away."

Helen cursed loudly as she dropped a piece of beetroot on her pink blouse. She hadn't even thought about the holiday season yet. Or what to get Kathy. Or where'd they'd spend it. Or just how she would survive the second anniversary of Meg's death that came before it.

Circumstance
Kate Charlton

"I hadn't thought about Christmas. I've got to figure out what to buy her. You're lucky you don't celebrate it. It's one less thing you have to worry about."

***

The clock chimed five times. Kathy looked up, then back down to the folder on her desk and closed it.

"Done." She was pleased with herself. She'd worked a little faster than she normally did to get finished early. She pulled her long woollen coat tightly around her slender body to keep out the chill that had descended upon London like a winter cape. A smile played on her lips as she thought about the weekend of Christmas shopping she had planned for herself and Doctor Scrooge, as she'd come to call Helen. It had turned into something of a long-running joke with the good doctor, ever since she'd been foolish enough to utter the eponymous Christmas Carol line within ear shot.

The lift screeched to a halt, its steel doors making a grinding sound as they opened. She swung her briefcase as she imagined just how she was planning on getting Helen into the mood. She dug her mobile out of her bag as she made her way down the hall, her heels echoed loudly on the concrete floor of the almost-empty multi-story building.

Circumstance
Kate Charlton

"Hey, baby!"

"Well, hello, sexy. Have you escaped?"

"I most certainly have! I'm just picking the car up now and then I'll be on my way!" A flash of movement caught Kathy's eyes and she stopped abruptly, her gaze darting around the empty floor.

"Are you there?" Helen asked, alarm building in her voice.

"I'm here. It was just my imagination." She quickly stepped towards her car and stopped as she got to the driver's side. "Oh, for fuck's sake! That fucking bitch…!" she yelled into the shadows.

"What? Talk to me, Kathy! What's happened?" The urgency made her voice sound distorted.

"She's gouged my fucking car again and left a dead fucking pigeon on my bonnet. Jesus!" Nausea crept into Kathy's belly and threatened to erupt into her throat.

"Go back inside and call the police."

"No, there's no point. They don't do anything."

"Then get in the car and get the fuck out of there. Stay on the line with me so I know you're okay."

Circumstance
Kate Charlton

Kathy used her gloved hand to swipe the dead pigeon off the bonnet and let herself into the car. There was no way of knowing how the poor bird had met its grisly end and she didn't particularly want to. She gunned the engine and threw the car into reverse, ready to be as far away from London as possible.

***

Loitering in the shadows, Petra Smythe watched it all. She'd slid up against a wall just in time to hide herself after Kathy exited the lift earlier than expected, phone clutched to her ear.

Keying the car had given her a rush of adrenaline. The pigeon had been an unexpected, but perfect, touch. She'd found the wounded bird in the corner of the car park, bleeding and close to death. It looked like it had been attacked and was certainly not a candidate for recovery, so putting it out of its misery was an act of mercy. She picked the bird up and regarded it for a few moments, watching with a morbid curiosity as its eyes grew dimmer by the second. In one swift movement, she took the bird's head in one hand, its body in the other, and quickly snapped its neck.

Kathy's reaction to her work had been almost beautiful—the way her face creased with disgust, the words sticking in her throat as the realisation hit her.

Circumstance
Kate Charlton

You're next, bitch.

***

Exhaustion took over as Kathy pulled into Helen's driveway, the glow of lamplight from inside the house warming her soul like balm. Helen must have heard the car because she came straight out, a torch in hand to inspect the damage to the car.

Kathy was relieved to see Helen's beautiful face. No matter how many times they travelled the long distance, it was always like seeing her for the first time. Strong arms pulled her close and she instantly felt at home.

"I suppose the word cunt makes a refreshing change to slut or bitch," she joked feebly.

Helen flashed the torch over the scratches and shook her head. "We'll take it to the body shop tomorrow and see if we can get it fixed up. I think we need to have a word with David, seeing as the police at your end are fucking useless."

They made their way to the cottage. Kathy kicked the front door closed behind her and followed Helen inside, straight to the kitchen. They'd developed a routine whenever Kathy arrived, where her lover would move gracefully to the fridge and pour them both a glass of wine.

Circumstance
Kate Charlton

"I don't want to talk about that woman this weekend!" Kathy stated, then wrapped her arms around Helen's neck. Helen tipped her head back.

Kathy leaned in and kissed her lover deeply, missing how she tasted. She moaned softly, adoring how her lover turned her on, no matter how grumpy or mad she was at outside influences. She pulled one of Helen's hands from around her waist and guided it to the hem of the skirt just above her knee. Helen's fingers traced higher, following the line of the garter holding Kathy's stockings in place.

Helen let out a loud moan as her hand slid up the silky skin.

Knowing exactly what she was doing to Helen, Kathy let out a small giggle.

Helen took her by the waist and lifted her onto the breakfast bar, the fabric of the tight skirt bunching around her hips.

"I thought I'd remind you what you're missing…." Kathy whispered.

Helen pushed her lover back until she was lying on the counter and pulled her legs up over her shoulders.

Circumstance
Kate Charlton

"Is that right? Driving all the way from London without underwear? You're a very bad girl," she drawled, stroking her thumb over Kathy's hard clit.

Kathy's eyes closed and a throaty moan escaped her parted lips.

"And just what do you plan on doing about that?" she managed to ask.

In response, Helen slid two fingers into her opening and immediately pulled back out, eliciting an even louder groan from her lover.

"I'm going to make you pay. Stay there. Don't move!" she commanded.

A huge smile spread across Kathy's face as she heard her lover take the stairs two at a time and cross into their bedroom. She knew exactly what she was in for....

Helen returned and pulled Kathy off the breakfast island. Their kisses were frantic, tongues fighting for control as they ripped at each other's clothes until fabric pooled on the cold tile beneath their feet. Slowly, Helen led her into the living room and lowered her down onto the sofa. Kathy licked her lips seductively and eyed the toy nestled between Helen's thighs. With slow deliberation, she wrapped her arms around her lover's neck. Her breath caught in her throat as long fingers sought her centre and opened her up, exposing her to Helen's throbbing need. Kathy grinned, her eyelashes fluttering as she took as much of her lover as she could.

Chapter 14

By mid-week, Helen felt useless. Normally she didn't take off from work, but her business partner kindly reminded her she was no use to the patients when she couldn't remain focused.

She'd dragged herself out of bed that morning after an endless night of tossing and turning. She'd been plagued by nightmares—Meg's face, repeatedly, distorted by pain and anguish. Meg's voice pleading with her to stop her from dying. Her passing hadn't been anything like that. It was peaceful and calm and in hospice, which they had chosen together. She wasn't sure what changed. The dreams were back, the same ones she'd had after Meg had died. Her own GP diagnosed her with post-traumatic stress. She'd foolishly self-medicated with booze until David had dragged her to see a counsellor who dealt with cognitive behavioural therapy, having pointedly told her that he was not going to let her kill herself.

She felt useless, not able to eat or sleep. Instead, she survived on coffee, and when that didn't help, she opened a bottle of Merlot and, once numb, climbed up into the loft and pulled down all the photo albums that chronicled their marriage over eighteen wonderful years. Her favourite picture of them would always be the one taken on a holiday in Portugal, about eight years before cancer had even reared its ugly head in their lives. The picture showed them standing together in front of an amazing sunset, arms around each other, very much in love.

***

David used his key to let himself into Helen's house after Kathy called and told him Helen wasn't answering her phone. The moment he entered the house, he could smell stale alcohol, and on the living room carpet he found her slumped over, surrounded by a myriad of photos with an empty bottle at her side.

"Come on, let's pack a bag for you. You're not staying here tonight. You're coming home with me."

"I'm okay, David."

"No, you aren't. If I have to carry you to the car, I will. Come on, you need to put some clothes on so I can get you out of here. Just for tonight."

Helen let herself be guided in the direction of her bedroom and silently sat on the bed as her brother packed her an overnight bag. Her head and heart ached. She slumped and hugged herself. Her thoughts continued to torment her, a heaviness filling her heart.

Circumstance
Kate Charlton

***

David's wife, Andrea, fed Helen chicken soup before putting her to bed in the spare room. She hated to see her sister-in-law looking so fragile and lost. She would give anything to make it better. Seeing Helen like this reminded her of when Meg first passed away. Helen had been Meg's rock throughout her brief illness, having been through this twice before. Not once had Andrea or David seen Helen show the slightest hint of emotion or distress whilst Meg had been alive. She admired how Helen arranged the hospital appointments, did the shopping, and paid the bills, all the while still working. Andrea remembered how she would enthuse over the essential oil massages that Meg enjoyed, and how they really did seem to revitalise her for a short time. It was one of the few things that made Helen smile in those couple of months. It was only after Meg's funeral that Helen began to unravel, first by not taking phone calls from family, and then taking time away from work, and then drinking to the point of passing out.

Andrea and David had made a point of visiting her every day, just to make sure that she was still there, terrified that Meg's death would tip her over the edge and she would try to do something silly. Instead, Helen had spent two months trying to slowly drink herself to death.

Circumstance
Kate Charlton

The breaking point had finally arrived on Valentine's Day, when Andrea called to check on Helen after work. She'd found her in the bathroom, naked except for a pair of shorts, and passed out. The bathroom floor and toilet were streaked with vomit, some clinging to her short blonde hair, filling the entire second floor with an acrid odour that burned Andrea's sinuses.

Andrea had called David and told him that enough was enough; Helen needed help. They'd managed to rouse the inebriated woman and put her under a cold shower, despite the screams and drunken abuse that she hurled directly at her family. They'd taken her home with them after sending the kids to Andrea's parents, and David held his sister in his arms until the grief and alcohol slowly left her body.

Helen stayed with her brother for another few weeks, finally allowing her family to care for her. She'd been lucky enough to get an emergency referral to a therapist who helped her to come to terms with her loss. She was finally able to wake up each morning without reaching for a bottle of alcohol. It was a gruelling, painful process, but she got through it.

***

Kathy had no idea what was going on and the unknown scared her.

Circumstance
Kate Charlton

"I'm so scared that she'll walk away from our relationship, Emma." Curled up on the corner of her sofa, she pulled her knees tight to her chest. "Maybe I sound like the most selfish person in the world, but I was just getting excited about our first Christmas together."

Emma patted her knee. "You need to give her time, Kathy. She's grieving, and as much as she's probably thought that things have gotten better, holidays and anniversaries are going to be hard for years to come."

Kathy's fingers plucked at a bobble of fabric on her grey sweats.

"What if she realises she can never love me as much as she loved Meg? I feel like I'm fighting a losing battle. How the fuck can I compete with a ghost, for god's sake?"

"Kathy, you need to stop this right now!" Emma demanded, pointing a cherry-red nail at her friend. "What ifs won't get you anywhere. You need to give her time and let her find her own way through this. You can't compare yourself to Meg. That's not fair to anyone and it will drive you insane. Helen loves you; any fool can see that when you two are together."

Kathy dug her fingers through her curls.

"I'm so scared of losing her. I love her so bloody much."

Emma pulled her into a hug and kissed her hair.

"I know you do, sweetie. It'll be okay, it's just all happening at a shitty time of year, and you've both got all sorts of things going on in your lives. Speaking of which, what did the police say about the latest incident with your car?"

"I didn't even bother to report it," she admitted in a small voice.

Emma pulled back to look at her. "Why the fuck not?"

"I was in a hurry and I just wanted to get to Helen's. What the hell would they have done about it? It would've taken them over an hour to get there and then it would take forever for them to collect evidence from the car, and I'd never have gotten to Newcastle!"

"She left a dead…fucking…pigeon on your bonnet!" Emma spoke as though addressing a small child.

"I know. I'm just so tired of it controlling my life. If I had to wait for the police every time I got a message or some sort of interaction, I'd never be able to go anywhere or do anything. They've spent so long on this, and where are we?"

Circumstance
Kate Charlton

"Sweetie, this woman has made escalating threats to kill you! Plus she's on the run from a secure facility! How much more horror film can this get before she finally snaps for good?"

Kathy laughed mirthlessly and poured them another glass of wine from the almost-empty bottle.

"Gee, you know how to pick a girl up when she's down!"

As much as she hated to admit it, Emma was right, but she still ached for the amazing woman who'd stolen her heart. She thought back to a conversation she'd once shared with her mother after experiencing her first heartbreak. She could picture her mother sitting at the enormous oak dining table in the kitchen of their converted farmhouse. Her mother was shelling pea pods, preparing to cook dinner as she always did. On hearing of her daughter's heartbreak, she'd given Kathy the best piece of advice by reminding her that true love should never be hard. *"That's not to say you won't experience hard times together, but how you deal with those hard times will be the test of true love. Your time will come, Kathy. One day, you will meet the love of your life and you'll know why all of your other relationships didn't work out."*

Circumstance
Kate Charlton

Kathy smiled fondly at the memory, remembering just how world-wise her mother had been. She would have had all the answers where Helen was concerned, and she'd have loved her lover too. Her mother had been right—it may have taken her until the age of forty-two, but now she knew why none of her other relationships had worked out.

***

Helen woke to what felt like a parade of soldiers marching through her skull. For a moment, she was disoriented, not recognising the single bed with the flowery chintz duvet cover, or the heavy oak furniture that adorned the room. She reached her hand out for the warm body beside her and found nothing but cold sheets. Her brain processed the information and the previous evening started to trickle back. She peeled her tongue from the roof of her mouth and gingerly rolled onto her back, hoping the movement wouldn't make her stomach revolt.

She scrunched her eyes and swallowed hard. This was all terrifyingly familiar. She couldn't go back to that. She'd worked too damned hard to survive and find her way into the world again. After Meg died, she'd wake each morning and reach for a warm body next to her. It had taken her months to break the habit, and she realised with utter surprise she'd done it again this morning. Except this time, it wasn't Meg she'd reached for, but Kathy. She sighed deeply as a thousand emotions washed over her all at once. Meg was gone and she would forever leave an enormous hole in Helen's heart, but she couldn't bring her wife back. Kathy was alive, vibrant, and completely and utterly in love with her.

And how did you deal with this, Kennedy? You got smashed, disappeared up your own arse, and ignored her for the whole damned day instead of talking about it like a reasonable adult. Fuck.

Cautiously, she pulled herself up into a sitting position and swung her legs around to the side of the bed, wincing as her headache intensified and her stomach threatened to eject its contents once again. Beads of sweat formed on her forehead, and she swallowed the nausea down for the second time.

"I'm too old for this shit!" she grumbled to the empty room.

She stumbled into the kitchen to find Andrea seated at the polished kitchen table, reading the broadsheet newspaper. Radio 4 played quietly in the background. Her sister-in-law folded the corner of the newspaper down and eyed her silently over the top of her reading glasses.

Circumstance
Kate Charlton

Helen sat down heavily, her elbows on the table and her head hung low as she suspiciously eyed the glass of fizzing liquid and the slimy abomination in the tumbler next to it.

"If I offer you my salary from next month, will you please let me off from drinking these?" she asked, her voice thick.

Andrea set her reading glasses down atop the now-folded newspaper on the table. "Sink the painkiller first, then you can enjoy your Prairie Oyster."

Helen eyed the glass of slime that seemed to stare back at her and her stomach lurched again. She'd hoped to never see another one of Andrea's amazing hangover cures: a raw egg, Worcestershire sauce, salt, and ground black pepper, all in the same glass and intended to be swallowed in one gulp. She remembered the first time Andrea had served it to her, a few weeks after they'd met and following a particularly raucous night out. She hadn't thought about it in a very long time. She gulped and threw the fizzing painkillers down her throat, holding her head back long after she'd swallowed to stop the liquid from coming back up. She shuddered and let out an animalistic moan.

"Serves you right!" Andrea admonished as she folded her arms across her chest.

Circumstance
Kate Charlton

Helen eyed her sister-in-law suspiciously, wondering if all social workers had this sadistic side to them. A smile played at the corner of Andrea's full lips.

"You like to torture me, don't you?"

"Drink your Oyster!" Andrea replied pointedly.

Helen continued to glare at the glass. "I remember the first time you made me one of these." She knew she was stalling and so did Andrea, who remained silent. "Did I drink that very first one?"

"You didn't have a choice. It was the only way I was ever going to get you well enough to get out of my flat after you'd spent the night hugging my toilet."

Helen held out her hands. "Hey, if it wasn't for me, you'd never have met or married my brother."

"Stop stalling. Drink the goddamned Oyster."

Helen knew that resistance was futile. She watched the slimy contents of the glass slither menacingly about. She closed her eyes and took a deep breath, then threw the cocktail down like a shot of tequila. The concoction slid down the back of her throat, making her gag violently until the Prairie Oyster was well on its way down her oesophagus. She banged her hand down hard on the tabletop and grimaced.

Circumstance
Kate Charlton

"Jesus, that was nasty!"

"What doesn't kill you makes you stronger," Andrea reminded her.

"May I please have some coffee now?" Helen practically begged.

Andrea glided gracefully around the spacious kitchen, preparing the coffee machine in silence. She always appeared cool and, at times, a little posh, though Helen knew the real woman under the façade was no such thing. "I remember the first night I met you, Helen said. "Twenty years old, legs that went up to your armpits, and an icy glare that could knock a guy dead at a hundred paces."

Andrea set the mug of coffee down on the table and returned to her seat.

"It didn't stop you from trying to get me into bed, no matter how much of a cold shoulder I gave you."

Helen blushed at the memory, glad that her brother didn't know about her very, very brief dalliance with his wife before they had been introduced to each other.

"You still preferred my brother in the end."

Andrea flashed a toothy grin, her face transforming with the new and unexpected expression.

Circumstance
Kate Charlton

"And you met Meg less than a year later and never looked back. It was a win-win. Now, on that perfect segue…." she prompted.

Helen sipped the hot coffee, the caffeine jolting her as the liquid burned her tongue. "Yesterday was tough, emotional, and I'm so sorry you had to take care of this drunken mess." She looked up, her eyes locking onto Andrea's impassive gaze.

"I know. No one ever expects Meg's anniversaries to be easy for you, but you can't hit the self-destruct button for every emotional crisis you skid into. David and I love you very much, and so does Kathy, who probably has absolutely no clue what's going on, the poor cow. I bet you didn't even speak to her yesterday, did you?"

Helen blushed, realising that Andrea knew her all too well.

"No. It hasn't been one of my finer moments, and I know I need to call her and explain."

Andrea arched an eyebrow, her head tilting slightly to one side as she took in the tiredness that etched deep lines around Helen's eyes. Her tone softened.

"Stop trying to take on the world and its disasters all on your own. You're not an infallible superhero, and there's no shame in voicing your emotions and asking for help. Don't be pulling that shit again."

Helen half smiled, staring down at her coffee cup in a crude attempt to avoid Andrea's blunt dressing-down.

"So, come on then, why did you go for David over me?" she asked with a teasing smile.

"Easy!" Andrea told her as she replaced her reading glasses and picked up the newspaper again. "He had a bigger cock."

Chapter 15

Helen stared at the cell phone in her hand and sighed. She'd lost her nerve and opted to text Kathy instead.

I'm sorry for being such an arse and disappearing on you. Are you still speaking to me? X

She wandered around her brother's house for half an hour, anxiously waiting for some sort of response, scared that her message would be met with silence. She knew she had a good thing—no, she had a great thing with Kathy, and the last thing she wanted to do was fuck it all up.

The crossword puzzle no longer held her interest. She pushed the paper to the side. On the table, her phone suddenly buzzed. She took a deep breath before picking it up and reading the message.

Can you talk? X

Yes, Helen quickly typed back.

Seconds later, the phone vibrated and Kathy's name flashed on the screen.

"Hi, you. Where are you?" Helen tried to sound as normal as possible and failed miserably.

Circumstance
Kate Charlton

"I'm just walking back to the office from court. I thought you were fucking dead, Helen!"

Helen pinched the bridge of her nose. "I'm sorry. I haven't handled this very well, have I? I didn't mean to push you out or hurt you. I suppose you have every right to be mad at me." She could hear the traffic in the background when Kathy became silent.

"I'm not mad, Helen. Disappointed that you couldn't talk to me? Yes. Upset that you made me worry myself half to death? Yes. I love you and I want to be able to take care of you, but I do understand why you did it."

Her understanding made Helen feel even more guilty. She picked up her cigarillos and lighter and headed out into the garden. Andrea would've killed her if she'd dared to light one in the house.

"I know," she said finally. "I'll make it up to you, I promise." She slumped backed in the iron chair, scraping its feet across the wooden deck.

"You don't need to make it up to me. Just talk to me."

"I will," Helen promised. She owed her girlfriend that much, and if she wanted the relationship to work out, it was time to pull her head out of her backside and make it happen.

Circumstance
Kate Charlton

***

When the call ended, Kathy stepped into the lift and pressed the button. She was relieved that Helen was okay, but the frustration and anger still lingered. Her mother's words about finding *The One* came back to her again and she realised that, despite Helen's shortcomings, she really did love her.

Helen was hers and hers alone and they would weather whatever storm that came their way. Quite simply, Kathy knew she couldn't live without her. That thought jolted her as she hung her long woollen coat on the back of her office door and smoothed down her suit jacket. No one had ever been her "forever" until Doctor Helen Kennedy came into her life.

***

Petra Smythe had no idea where she was driving or how long the journey would take, but she'd seen Kathy disappear for enough weekends at a time to know that she headed somewhere out of the area. She wondered if it was to see her fancy woman who didn't seem to be around all the time.

She'd filled the Micra's tank in anticipation of a long trip, and was glad she'd bothered. She'd been driving for over two hours. All she knew was that they were heading

Circumstance
Kate Charlton

northbound on the A1. It was taking all her concentration to keep Kathy in her sights. The Audi ahead of her was able to travel a lot more smoothly than her little junker. Her eyes were growing more and more tired, but she knew the journey would be worth it in the end, wherever it led. She chuckled to herself as she drove, the radio cranked and playing the latest travel news. *We're going on a magical mystery tour!*

After a little over five hours, Petra found herself in Newcastle upon Tyne, with its famous green half-moon bridge and the Sage Arts Venue glimmering like a giant silver condom in the night. Another fifteen minutes, and Petra slowed as she watched Kathy turn onto a well-hidden driveway just off the main road. She parked in front of a row of houses a little further on and watched to see if the car re-emerged. After half an hour passed, she was satisfied that this was where the mystery woman lived.

Dressed all in black, Petra crept down the winding driveway, using the shadows of bushes and trees to hide her from the moonlight. She stopped short when she saw the chocolate-box house at the end of the drive with Kathy's car parked on the gravel. She scanned the windows to see which were lit and which weren't, which showed signs of life and which didn't. Sticking to the tree line, she moved as close as she could until movement in one of the rooms caught her eye. Through the blinds, she could make out two entwined figures.

Looks like I've found your hidey-hole, you silly little bitch.

***

Kathy loved being consumed in Helen's strong yet tender embrace. Her lover's fragrance made her feel like she was home. She let her tongue tease Helen's, flicking over her bottom lip and eliciting low groans when she plunged her tongue into her mouth. *Jesus, I can't get enough of her.* She pulled back so they could both catch their breath. They had quite a bit of air to clear between them first. The last thing Kathy wanted was for them both to lapse back into their version of normalcy with unresolved questions and issues hanging in the air.

"Come on," she said, taking Helen gently by the hand. "Let's go and get comfortable."

***

Helen absentmindedly rubbed the small feet nestled in her lap and stared into the dying embers of the log fire. It was well past 2 a.m. and the two of them had talked themselves hoarse about their fears and dreams, stopping only to lubricate themselves with Pinot. The one thing they both realised was that, as much as they were both unnerved by the intensity of their new relationship, they were even more concerned about the prospect of losing it.

Kathy admitted her fears of having to compete with a ghost, and how she was afraid Helen could never love her that much. They both cried, and Kathy listened patiently as Helen talked about Meg and the life that they'd shared.

"You are two totally different people," Helen explained gently. "And, yes, I loved her with all of me." She paused, then swirled the dark liquid around in her glass, watching it coat the sides before taking a sip. "But I'm one of the lucky few. My heart grew back and it beats bigger and stronger than ever. I'm able to love *you* with all of me, too."

Kathy, overcome with emotion, hadn't been able to reply. Helen lay on her back, her hair spread out on the cushion behind her head, her empty glass cradled on her stomach. *She looks so beautiful in profile*, she thought as the orange embers reflected in Kathy's eyes.

"What are you thinking?" Kathy asked.

Helen took a deep breath. It was as if the weight of the world had been lifted off her shoulders.

"I'm thinking that I'm an extremely lucky woman to have the chance at true love twice in my life, and what a dolt I can be sometimes!" She broke into a smile and squeezed Kathy's toes. "Come on, lady, time for bed."

***

Helen's fingers slid up and down the fretboard of the seashore metallic burst Ibanez bass guitar. She made the instrument sing, her foot tapping in time to the basic rock rhythm. It was the first time Kathy had seen her wield the instrument, let alone heard her play, but something about the way the bass almost became a part of her was a massive turn on.

Helen put the bass down and wiped the strings gently. This, she'd told Kathy, was her baby. Tonight would be the first gig of hers that Kathy attended. It made her both nervous and excited.

Kathy plucked a peach from the wooden fruit bowl on the living room table and bit into the succulent, ripe flesh. The juices coated her lips, and she watched Helen's eyes darken with lust. She abandoned the instrument in the case and closed the distance between them, music long-forgotten, and pushed Kathy back against the sofa.

Kathy gasped and giggled in surprise.

"Maybe I should eat fruit with you more often! Time for an afternoon nap?" she asked coyly.

Circumstance
Kate Charlton

***

From her car, Petra Smythe stretched her tired muscles. She was afraid to let Kathy out of her sight. She wanted to see everything Kathy was doing with this bitch behind Anna's back. *I'll make them both pay!*

The car wasn't exactly comfortable to spend so much time in, but at least she had dressed for the elements in plenty of layers, and there was a small supermarket and café nearby to get plenty of coffee and snacks. She felt like a cop on a stake-out. The thought made her giggle. No one seemed to notice her parked there, or if they had, they didn't approach her. It was nice to know that people in the North paid just as little attention to what went on around them as those in the South. It suited her purpose just fine.

By six in the evening, she was beginning to think that nothing was going to happen for the rest of the day. Kathy and Helen hadn't left the house and the only exit was the winding driveway. Just as she was thinking of giving up for the night and booking herself a comfortable bed somewhere, an estate car slowed and turned down the concealed driveway. Petra sat forward in her seat to get a better look.

Circumstance
Kate Charlton

Chapter 16

Once the car was loaded with all the gear and instruments, Helen turned to Kathy and introduced her bandmate Christine and her wife Heather. Kathy sat in the back with Heather, the younger partner by fifteen years. She was small and lithe with a cascade of blonde hair that made her look more like a movie star than a fellow GP.

"How did you two meet?" she asked.

Christine giggled from the driver's seat and looked back in the rear-view mirror at her wife. "You can tell this one, babe!"

Heather sighed. "When I qualified as a GP, I got my first job at Christine's surgery. I was twenty-eight and engaged to a guy I'd trained with. The wedding was booked for the day after my thirtieth birthday and I had my whole wonderful life planned, as you do when you hit that age and your dream career is finally a reality. Anyway, I was new and naïve and Christine was my mentor, and I just thought she was such an incredible doctor. I hung on her every word and ended up with a real hero worship complex. Before I knew it, it turned into an almighty crush. It completely messed with my head for a few months because, as far as I was concerned, I was straight and I'd found the guy I wanted to spend my life with. I thought that if I didn't say anything about it to anyone, it would go away and everything would be fine. Until we went to a conference one weekend." She paused and rested a hand on her partner's shoulder. "To cut a long story short, we had quite a bit to drink on the first night and ended up in bed together after too much whisky had given her the Dutch courage to tell me she'd developed feelings for me. We ended up having an affair for three months until I realised that I couldn't go on like that forever—it just wasn't fair to anyone. So, I went home from work one Friday night and told my fiancée everything. He was understandably devastated but I couldn't keep pretending. I moved in with Christine that night and fifteen years later, we're still blissfully happy together!"

"Wow!" And Kathy had thought her last relationship was dramatic. They seemed so happy together, though.

Heather chucked throatily. "Yeah, we get that reaction a lot! Oh, look, we're here!"

The car came to a stop in the pub car park. Kathy felt giddy. She couldn't wait to watch her sexy girlfriend command the stage.

***

Circumstance
Kate Charlton

The Micra pulled into the car park shortly after them and parked at the far side. The four women unloaded all the musical equipment from the boot.

Kathy didn't know whether to feel jealous or proud as women of all ages flocked around the band, particularly when they paid attention to Helen in her form-fitting t-shirt and slim black jeans. She looked the epitome of a rock star with her hair spiked and her slightly-darker-than-usual eyeshadow and mascara.

She remembered Helen mentioning the band in Rhodes, but she'd left out the part about the whole band being made up of lesbians who had quite the cult following! *Who knew there were so many lesbian GPs in this area!*

The back room of the lesbian-owned pub was decked out for Christmas, with tinsel everywhere and a massive tree in one corner of the cavernous room. It seemed that Dry Bones was a huge draw for a large portion of the Northeast's queer women. Kathy sipped her wine casually and watched a girl who couldn't have been more than thirty flirting shamelessly with Helen as she untangled leads and moved agilely around the equipment to set up. A cold finger of jealousy ran down her spine.

Heather noticed Kathy's change in demeanour and scooted her heavy old pub chair closer.

Circumstance
Kate Charlton

"I was in the same boat when I got together with Christine. These girls have been playing together for the best part of twenty years and have built up quite a fan base. I've known people who travel to see their gigs. It took me at least two years to lose the desire to choke the shit out of every woman who tried it on with Christine."

Kathy gave her a sideways glance.

"What changed?" she asked, her eyebrow raised.

Heather looked towards the stage, where a couple of women were chatting with her own wife. "Watch them both for a minute, yours and mine."

Kathy did, her gaze returning to the tableau in front of her. The young perky woman gave Helen all her attention and the two other women did their best to flirt with Christine.

"What do you see?" Heather prompted.

Kathy's eyes continued to scan the scene.

"I don't know." She shrugged half-heartedly.

"Okay, I'll spell it out for you. The women up there, our two women, are devoted to us, and they come home to us at the end of every gig. If you watch the way they interact with the hard-core groupies and the women who fancy their chances, you'll see that that's not how they interact with us. Sure, they're polite and they're friendly because the women pay to see them, but the mask they put on when they're on stage is no different to the mask they put on in front of their patients, and you don't worry about that, do you?"

Kathy's lips curled into a slow smile, her face burning in embarrassment.

"Have you ever thought about switching general medicine for psychology?" she teased.

Heather winked and picked their glasses up for a refill. Kathy watched in amazement. *She's a wise woman.*

When the set-up was finally complete, the band took the stage. Kathy took a hearty swig of her drink as they launched into the first strains of Melissa Etheridge's "Yes I Am".

She watched Helen close her eyes, lost to the beat, her fingers moving languidly over the frets of the slow-burner. Christine belted out the lyrics in the way only she could, and the crowd lapped it up.

Helen opened her eyes and scanned the audience until her gaze fell on Kathy. It was obvious, as Helen winked, that she could have had the pick of any groupie she wanted, but she'd chosen Kathy instead. The knowledge made her proud. *You all might want her, but she's coming home with me.*

***

Helen and Kathy were exhausted by the time they managed to get in the car. It took a little over an hour to pack up the equipment.

As the car pulled off the road and into the drive, Kathy's phone vibrated with a text message. She shifted in her seat to extricate the device from her snug jeans and squinted to read the display. *I really do need to buy some reading glasses.*

Her blood ran cold as she took in each word.

How are you enjoying Newcastle?

The car slowed to a stop and she heard Helen gasp. She looked up, heart pounding. On the front door, spray-painted in black, were the words 'cheating bitches'.

"Fucking bitch!" Helen ground out through clenched teeth, her hands balling into fists by her sides.

Kathy grabbed Helen's shoulder, the phone still clutched in her hand. "She knows I'm here. I got a text. She's followed me, Helen." Her voice shook as she scanned the line of trees around the perimeter of the house.

Circumstance
Kate Charlton

Kathy had nowhere left to go.

***

Christine and Heather helped them unload the equipment into the house and insisted upon staying until they knew Helen and Kathy were safe. Kathy and Heather were told to stay put in the kitchen whilst the two other women scanned every room of the house to make sure that Petra hadn't gotten in. Even though the house alarm had been set and not disturbed, they were too on edge to take the risk.

For tonight, they would hole up in the house, where they were safe, but Helen knew she'd reached boiling point with the crazy woman who had infested their lives like a disease. If anyone knew what to do, it would be David, and she would be calling him first thing in the morning.

Circumstance
Kate Charlton

Chapter 17

The next afternoon, Kathy stormed down the hall, her cell phone pressed against her ear. Determination echoed in each step of her high heels as they clicked against the floor, sharp as the crack of a whip. Her usual routine disregarded, she threw her coat over her arm and snatched her briefcase.

"Hi, Helen. It's me. I'm going home and packing enough clothes to last me for the next couple of weeks. I'm grabbing the next train and getting the fuck out of the city."

"Sweetheart, what happened?" Helen urged.

"I'll explain it all when I get there but I'm not driving. I'm taking a moonlight flight far away from the disaster that is my fucking life right now!"

She stabbed at the button to call the lift, her anger rising in her throat as she fought the urge to punch the nearest object. "I'll let you know when I'm on my way and you can pick me up from the station."

***

Circumstance
Kate Charlton

Kathy's plan felt like something from a noire film. She parked her car in the apartment car park and checked it twice to make sure it was locked. She threw her keys into her handbag and pulled out her phone, swiping the screen to access her contacts as she shouldered open the door into the building. She cursed when she lost the signal in the lift. Kathy tapped her foot impatiently as she waited for it to make its slow ascent. She redialled Michael as soon as she stepped into her apartment. Just as she was about to hang up, his chirpy greeting assaulted her. Luckily for her, he hadn't left for one of his many glamourous Christmas soiree events. Half an hour later, he arrived at her door, dressed in a midnight blue tuxedo with a matching bow tie.

"Because you aren't going to stand out in a crowd as my getaway driver!" Kathy smirked as she threw her clothes into a purple suitcase that lay open on her bed.

Michael idled against the doorframe, his hands in his pockets. He shrugged. "What can I say, princess? I have a champagne reception at seven for yet another high-end boutique looking for magazine space, and it's now six-fifteen and you need my help to escape. So get your mighty fine arse into gear and let's get going!" He snapped his fingers in the air, just above her head.

Circumstance
Kate Charlton

Kathy made a final visual sweep of her wardrobe and drawers and nodded in approval. The place looked as though a hurricane had blown through, with work suits now hanging in disarray and empty coat hangers on the wardrobe floor. She had everything she needed, and if she didn't, she could sure as hell buy it.

***

"Remind me again why you're paying exorbitant train fares instead of driving?" Michael asked, tapping his fingertips in time to the rhythm of the song playing on the radio.

"Because I have a crazy fuck-nut stalking me the length and breadth of the fucking country, my boss has put me on garden leave because that bitch thinks it's fun to try and trash my career, and all I want, for four fucking hours of my life, is a little bit of goddamned peace!" she yelled.

Michael gave her a sideways glance as he approached yet another red light.

"Better?" he asked timidly.

"Much," she murmured.

Michael reached over and patted her thigh.

Circumstance
Kate Charlton

"It'll all be okay, Kath. You'll see. We're going to have an amazing Northern Christmas together and forget about all of this crap."

Kathy adjusted her position in the passenger seat so she could see her best friend clearly, her dark curls draped over the collar of her woollen coat.

"I wouldn't miss that for the world, Mikey," she replied gently.

Kathy's face brightened into a genuine smile. No matter what she faced in her life, she felt like the luckiest woman in the world to have the love of the people around her. She took a deep breath and dispelled the anger that'd burned away at her insides for the past couple of hours. What she needed was a cheap trashy book to read on the train and a couple of gin-and-tonics to calm her nerves. Just the thought of it made her feel a little bit better.

Before she could open the car door, Michael reached over and kissed her cheek.

"Say the word and I'm there."

"I know, and I love you." As she opened the door, the uneasy feeling she'd had before returned. She looked around the parking lot. Several cars were parking and a few were driving through the gate. "Watch my back while

I make it through the doors. I have a feeling we were followed."

***

Helen gripped her steering wheel tightly as she navigated the myriad one-way streets out of Newcastle city centre. It was nearing midnight and the streets were packed full of revellers intent on kicking off their weekend in style. She crawled past the throngs of drinkers who waited to get into the Riverside nightclub, most of whom had consumed their body weight in alcohol. She stole a glance at Kathy, who'd finally relaxed in the passenger seat beside her; she was still dressed in her work suit and cream-colored woollen coat. She rested her elbow on the windowsill, propping her chin in her palm.

"Are you going to tell me what this is all about, now that you're here?" Helen probed.

Kathy stared straight ahead. "Take me somewhere calm and quiet and I'll tell you."

Helen drove the gauntlet that was the A189, with its endless traffic lights. A taxi pulled out in front of her and she slammed on her brakes. She honked the horn aggressively and shouted abuse as the taxi driver gave her the finger. *Fucking ignorant ass*. They both relaxed as the traffic calmed and the city centre disappeared in the rear-view mirror. The concrete and glass of the city gave way to dark open fields. Signs of life re-emerged as they drove into Jesmond and the orange streetlights lit their way. Helen pulled the car into the carpark at Jesmond Dene and the two women exited the car in silence. Helen grabbed a torch and blanket from the boot and locked the car.

Hand-in-hand, they silently walked the wooded trail, their boots crunching on the frosty ground, led by nothing but the dim beam of the torch. The woodland was alive with the sound of nocturnal wildlife. An owl screeched in a tree ahead of them and a fox barked somewhere behind them. Yet, at the same time, the swoosh of traffic in the distance as it ran the coast road reminded her they weren't far from civilization.

Helen pulled the collar of her waxed jacket more closely around her neck, trying to keep out the winter chill. The sky was crystal clear, sparkling with millions of brilliant stars. The freezing fog burned her lungs, but if this was what Kathy needed, she didn't care how cold it got.

They followed the path until they came to the waterfall that ran under the footbridge. There was no noise, except for the splash of water on rocks.

"Stop here," Kathy instructed. "This place is perfect."

Circumstance
Kate Charlton

They found a spot on a boulder at the side of the river and nestled into one another. Kathy closed her eyes for a few moments, like she was rallying her courage.

"I've been suspended from work."

Helen frowned deeply and looked down at the silhouette of her lover. "What on earth do you mean, suspended? What did they say you've done?"

Kathy wrapped her arms tightly around her body and bit back a sob.

"The allegation is that I sexually harassed a woman who worked in a client's office I visited between March and April. It's a total fabrication. I've never even heard of this woman, and the only secretary in that office was an older woman who would let the client know I was there and walk me to the office!" Her eyes filled with tears. She swiped them away roughly with her coat sleeve and sniffed.

"Why would someone even think of doing something like that?" Helen demanded. "That's just craziness. What did your boss say? And why in hell did he suspended you?"

Kathy took another deep breath. "He has to follow protocol whether there's any truth to an allegation or not. I don't blame him for that, but I want him to get to the bottom of this sooner rather than later. I spent the whole journey up here racking my brain. Am I a magnet for complete psychopaths or what?"

Helen held out her hands for Kathy to take and then pulled her up into a tight hug, placing a soft kiss to her forehead.

"We'll get to the bottom of it and it'll all disappear once she's found out as a lying bitch." She pulled back so she could see Kathy's face properly. "Come on, let's get you home before you catch hypothermia out here."

Kathy let Helen take her by the hand and lead her back onto the trail. When she spoke, her voice was so soft that Helen almost didn't hear her.

"I thought… I thought you might not believe me. I thought you might ask me to leave," she whispered. Helen squeezed her hand.

"Never."

***

The aroma of essential oils relaxed Kathy as she leaned back in Helen's oversized tub. Helen insisted that she soak when they got back to the house. Kathy loved the bathroom. It was as big as the master bedroom but looked even bigger due to the all-white design: white subway tiles that ran halfway up the walls, white appliances, and the enormous bath built into the alcove below three narrow windows. Hot water lapped over her naked flesh, plumes of steam rising into swirls like ghosts above her.

Helen came through the bathroom door, a glass of wine in each hand. She bent down and kissed Kathy softly, then made herself comfortable on the curved teak shower seat and leaned back against the wall.

"Is the bath relaxing you?"

Kathy gratefully sipped her wine and nodded, gingerly placing her glass on the side of the tub before sinking back into the foamy bubbles "Definitely." Her eyes roamed over Helen's lithe body and lingered longer than she'd planned on the tanned cleavage just visible above the vee of her heavy denim jacket.

"Why don't you get undressed and join me in here?" She blinked with feigned innocence.

A languid smile curved Helen's lips as she got up slowly and stood at the side of the bath.

She knelt, her sleeves rolled up past her elbows, and let her fingers trace lazily over the slick flesh of Kathy's abdomen.

"Are you wanting me to scrub your back?" she teased.

"Not quite what I had in mind," Kathy drawled as the exploring fingers made her abdomen tense.

Helen teased lower, fingers lightly brushing over Kathy's smooth skin. She listened to her lover sigh deeply with pleasure as her eyes concentrated on Helen's roaming fingers. She moved them lower, stroking upwards over Kathy's clit. She gasped.

"You're such a fucking tease," Kathy moaned, her own fingers moving down her body to encourage Helen to keep going.

"Tell me what you want," Helen asked quietly.

Their eyes locked.

"You know what I want." Her arm snaked up around Helen's neck and she pulled her down for a deep lingering kiss.

Helen stood and quickly stripped out of her clothes, throwing them carelessly out of the way. She stepped into the steaming water and lowered herself gently before pulling Kathy into her arms. Kathy slid onto Helen's lap and kissed her hard, moaning as Helen's fingers found her aching centre. She rocked her hips against Helen's hand, urging the probing fingers deeper inside her. Kathy tossed

Circumstance
Kate Charlton

her head back, inviting Helen to suck on the pale flesh of her exposed throat. Helen's fingers matched Kathy's urgent rhythm as she took her harder, her thumb pressed against Kathy's swollen clit.

She roared as the orgasm crashed over her, rendering her completely speechless. Helen wrapped her arms around Kathy's shaking body and kissed her chest. Neither woman moved as they revelled in the moment, glad to be back in each other's embrace.

***

Helen strode around the kitchen, pulling ingredients from the fridge for a simple salad for work, taking gulps of coffee as she went. She'd told Kathy that she had never been particularly good at getting out of bed on time in the morning and always ended up rushing around to get things done.

Kathy shook her head, unable to stop herself from laughing at the scene before her.

"I'll make sure you come home to a nice dinner tonight," she said, resting her chin on her upturned palm.

Helen kissed her on the lips, coffee in one hand and a carton of tomatoes in the other.

"That would be nice."

Circumstance
Kate Charlton

Her low heels echoed on the tile floor as she marched back to the kitchen counter.

"Will you be okay on your own all day?" she threw back over her shoulder.

"Of course I will. I'm a big girl and I can take good care of myself. I might catch the Metro into city centre and finish my Christmas shopping. I usually finish it on my way home from the office on Christmas Eve!" she admitted. "I need to ring work this morning, too. I have to find out what's happening with everything. I know it sounds stupid, seeing as I'm a solicitor, but would you help me write my statement tonight? You're more objective than I can be."

Helen clicked the lid onto her Tupperware box, eyes scanning the kitchen.

"Of course I will, honey." She stuffed the box into her briefcase. "Aha!" She grabbed her navy-blue suit jacket from the back of the chair, finally pausing to give Kathy her full attention. "I hate leaving you alone all day. I feel like I'm abandoning you."

Kathy sighed. The last thing she wanted was to complicate Helen's life.

"Helen, I'm fine, I promise. That's why I did a moonlit flight this way. It wouldn't have been easy to follow me here, so I think I'm safe. She has before, though. But I don't think even Petra would drive all the way up here on the off-chance that she'd find me."

Helen frowned.

"Don't underestimate her, Kathy. She's mentally unwell, clearly going through a psychotic break, and is very dangerous. She's not going to get bored and move on."

"I'm aware of that after all these years, thank you!" She rolled her shoulders in her thick white dressing gown and sipped coffee from the mug she cradled in both hands. "I'm sorry, I know you're just worried about me. I shouldn't have snapped."

Helen stepped closer and draped her arms around Kathy's shoulders. She planted a gentle kiss on the tip of her nose.

"It's okay. I'm sorry, too. I slip into doctor mode a bit too easily at times. Go out and have a nice day. Worry as little as possible about work and relax. Treat yourself."

Kathy patted her gently on the chest. "Go and save lives, Doc. Call or message me when you can if it'll put your mind at ease. I love you."

Circumstance
Kate Charlton

"I love you, too." Helen kissed her lips, and Kathy savoured the taste of coffee and happiness. Helen picked up her things and left the kitchen. A moment later, she heard the front door slam.

Kathy watched Helen slide into her car and crank it up. She pulled a U-turn, and her tail-lights disappeared behind the hedge. She took a moment to readjust to the silence before draining her coffee mug and making her way to the shower.

Chapter 18

Petra Smythe sat on an old tan leather sofa in the small flat she'd managed to secure using someone else's ID. It was still dark out. She stared into oblivion through the window until shapes and colours appeared in the nothingness. The fingers of her right hand irritated a loose thread in the seat's stitching. It amazed her that there were still landlords out there who weren't too interested in background checks and references. They didn't care who a tenant was, as long as the rent was paid on time every month.

She looked around the sparsely furnished flat with a sense of detachment. It wasn't a home. It was merely a base, with one small bedroom just big enough to fit a double bed and a set of drawers. The only items that made the place look lived in were the remnants of last night's feast. She'd worked her way through a bag of potato chips with dip, a quart of ice cream, and a full packet of cookies, but none of it had helped. Even the half-litre bottle of vodka she'd started hadn't kept the demons at bay as it usually did. Nothing filled the intense loneliness that overwhelmed her. Everyone in her life abandoned her in the end, no matter how hard she tried to keep them. That was why she couldn't walk away from Anna.

Circumstance
Kate Charlton

She broke down into uncontrollable sobs. She felt like the only person left in the world. She missed Anna desperately.

Finally, she sat upright and took a deep breath. She couldn't allow herself to fall apart, or they really would need to put her back into the psychiatric facility.

"Pull yourself together," Petra snapped. She jumped off the couch. She needed to get her hair trimmed, and it would do her good to get out of this claustrophobic apartment for a while.

She locked up behind her and made her way down the street to the hairdresser's shop. She stopped as she caught her reflection in the window. She no longer recognized herself. At one time, she'd had long hair. Her mother had never allowed her to cut it. Her words still lingered in Petra's mind: *"Real young ladies have long, lustrous locks to impress the men."*

Petra smirked. Those words were the main reason she was going to cut her hair.

Prior to her father's death, life was wonderful. Each day, she'd run to greet him when he came home from work and throw herself into his arms. *Daddy's girl*, he'd always called her. She often thought that her mother was a little jealous of how close the two of them were, even though her father obviously adored his wife and was never afraid of showing his affection for her.

Petra remembered the day the police arrived on the doorstep. It had been shortly after nine in the evening. They stood on the stoop, hats in their hands, and all she heard was her mother scream. Petra ran down the stairs to listen, the smell of wood polish hanging heavily in the air from the housekeeper's efforts earlier in the day. She'd heard the words *train, jumped, suicide,* and watched her mother crumple to the floor with a wail. Petra simply returned to her bedroom and cried herself to sleep, unable to comprehend the fact that she'd never see the man who'd been her lifelong idol again. Even now, she couldn't remember if her mother had ever told her that her father had died. It was something that they never spoke of, even on the day of his funeral. There had been no rational reason or explanation as to why he'd killed himself—no suicide note, no inkling that there had been anything wrong. That uncertainty had stayed with her for the rest of her life.

Her mother became a different woman within six months of his death, leaving a young Petra with no one to protect her. When she would come home from school, she smelled brandy on her mother's breath when she kissed her hello. The first time she knew everything had changed for good, it had been a Saturday night. She had to go to the bathroom at the end of the hall past her mother's bedroom. She'd heard grunts coming from behind the closed door.

When she got to the door, she crouched down low, flattening herself against the oak bannister rails so she could see through the key hole. Her mother was lying flat on her back, her legs over the shoulders of Daddy's best friend while his white bottom thrust back and forth. Petra knew what sex was, of course, but she had never seen it. The sight sickened her, but she was unable to tear herself away until the drunken couple had finished and began to move. She remembered the mixed feelings of revulsion and fascination as she remained glued to the spot, and how, every time she heard noises in the darkness, she'd creep out of her bedroom to see which man it was on that particular night.

By the time she left the hairdresser, another little part of the old Petra Smythe had disappeared, and the new Juliet Harker was taking shape. Gone was the long blonde hair she'd had since childhood, and in its place was a sleek, jaw-length chestnut bob. She held her head up high and threw back her shoulders. She could be anything she wanted to be and do anything she set her mind to. It was her survival method in the life that had been thrust upon her.

Chapter 19

Helen speared an ear of baby sweetcorn and popped it into her mouth, groaning with pleasure at Kathy's culinary skills.

"I could get used to coming home to a gorgeous woman and a home-cooked meal every night," she teased, her spare hand toying with the rim of her wine glass.

It was so nice to sit together in the cosy dining room, the table set for two and a large candle casting shadows that danced across Kathy's features.

"Have you heard anything from work today?" Helen asked.

Kathy dabbed the corner of her mouth with a cream-colored cotton napkin and shook her head.

"No. Nothing important, anyway. Just an email from Alex saying that he'd commenced a formal investigation. I said I'd have my statement to him by end of the day tomorrow. I've also been in touch with the Law Society for advice, for whatever good that does. Considering we're a legal profession, it always feels a bit ridiculous that we don't have a union as such." She smiled at Helen's empty plate as she stacked it on top of her own.

"Were they very helpful?"

Kathy gave a lopsided shrug.

"Not really." Her mouth quirked up on one side, as though she had an itch. "It's crazy that I know I'm innocent and that there is nothing to answer for yet I'm still worried."

Helen reached across the table and took her hand.

"I know, but it'll soon be over and sorted. You just have to wait it out. I've got every faith in a quick resolution."

Kathy stood, dropping a kiss onto the top of Helen's head.

"I know. I love you. Let's have some cheesecake in the living room to cheer ourselves up!"

Helen leaned back in her chair as Kathy sauntered into the kitchen, the firm round shape of her behind looking fantastic in form-fitting jeans.

***

Petra Smythe, or Juliet Harker, as she was called today, sat in Alex Falsom's office, looking the epitome of demure and professional in a black polo, slim-fitting black slacks, and a heavy black military-style coat. She held her hands clasped in her lap, her left leg crossed over her right, playing the role of victim to perfection. She had no need to acknowledge the secretary taking notes who sat in the leather chesterfield office chair across the room; she just had to get her well-rehearsed story straight.

"Now, Miss Harker, you understand that I have an obligation to investigate any complaints made in relation to my employees. I understand that this is probably a very stressful time for you and I do appreciate you taking time to come and see me on such short notice." His eyes roamed over her toned, curvaceous figure appreciatively.

Creep, she thought. He was blatantly obvious.

"I understand that, Mr. Falsom. I just want a quick resolution."

He nodded slowly while he considered her response, then slid his black-rimmed reading glasses over his ears and cast a glance over her written statement.

"I'll explain the process that this investigation will take and if you have any questions, I'll answer them as honestly as I can. Alright?"

She said nothing.

"Good. Okay, so I've already been through Miss Harland's employment record, the details of which you're not privy to, and I will be asking your former employer if they'd be so kind as to provide us with some information also."

"I understand." She didn't care that her 'former employer' would have no record of Juliet Harker; this was all about playing the game.

Alex frowned as he removed his glasses and sat ramrod-straight in his high-backed chair. "What outcome are you seeking, Miss Harker?" He rolled his thumbs slowly around each other.

Petra dipped her head slightly so that she could look up at him, making herself look like a victim who was embarrassed at having to answer.

"Like I told you in my statement, Mr. Falsom, I was an outgoing, bubbly person prior to this string of incidents, but Miss Harland's actions have obliterated my self-esteem. I had to leave a job I loved because I was terrified that she'd come back to the office one day, which also affected my relationship. I think the only reasonable outcome that'd be acceptable to me would be Miss Harland's dismissal."

Alex pursed his lips and glanced to his secretary.

"Very well, Miss Harker. The point of today's meeting with you is so that we can obtain your statement for our records, in addition to the written one you've already sent me. I'll also ask your former employer to send us any information he can obtain, and statements from anyone you're able to think of who may have seen Miss Harland's alleged actions first-hand."

Petra played along. She had all the time in the world and she was beginning to enjoy herself. She readjusted her position and re-crossed her legs, slowly enough to grab Alex's attention again.

After an hour and a half, the meeting finally ended. Petra could see the effect she'd had on Alex, the way his eyes were constantly drawn to her full breasts and heart-shaped mouth. Her plan was working, so she flicked her tongue over her lower lip when his eyes were trained on her.

The secretary had already left by the time she'd put her coat back on and collected her belongings. She allowed him to walk her to the office door, his body half-blocking it as he held the handle with one hand and offered his other to shake. Petra took it, letting her thumb slide over the back of his wrist.

"Thank you for coming in, Miss Harker," Alex murmured. His tone had become low and seductive.

"My pleasure," she drawled, shooting him a seductive grin. "It's such a shame about the circumstances. Maybe if they'd been different…." She let the sentence hang in the air.

Alex Falsom blushed as he held the office door open for her. She felt his gaze linger on the disappearing figure of Juliet Harker as she sashayed away down the corridor.

***

The next few days passed in a blur. David and Andrea extended an invitation to Kathy for a dinner party at their home on Wednesday evening, which she eagerly accepted. She adored spending time with Helen every day, but she was a woman who was used to being constantly busy and Christmas shopping and gift wrapping just wasn't enough for her. Kathy had even begun to work her way through Helen's book collection in between cleaning the house from top to bottom and making dinner to welcome Helen home from work. Adult company was exactly what she needed right now, and a small dinner party sounded heavenly.

On the evening of the party, Helen wandered into the bedroom, naked except for the towel thrown around her shoulders that she used to dry her hair. Kathy grinned as she flung her arms around Helen's neck and kissed her.

Circumstance
Kate Charlton

"Mmm, I think I could enjoy having you as an appetiser."

Helen moaned into her mouth, but she pulled back.

"Honey, you can't let me go to my brother's house in soaked jeans and undies! It simply isn't fair!" she whispered.

Kathy flicked her tongue over her teeth and raised an eyebrow coyly. "You wouldn't if you let me finish what I started!"

Helen kissed her deeply again.

"I'll compromise. You can have me for dessert instead!" She fished a clean pair of underwear out of the drawer and stepped into them as Kathy enjoyed the floor show.

"I hope your sister-in-law likes me. I'm not sure I know much about social work. What am I supposed to make conversation about?" she asked, her hands twisting in her lap.

"Oh, Andrea is a person of many talents and interests. I'm sure she'll do all of the talking and you'll just have to keep up," Helen replied. "Besides, you're just her type!" Helen winked and laughed as she buttoned up her blouse.

Kathy took a second look to ensure she'd put her makeup back into her clutch bag.

"What do you mean?" she demanded.

"Andrea's bi—not that David knows. He'd have a heart attack. Seriously, though, she adores him and her days of loving 'em and leaving 'em ended when she met him." Helen finished buttoning up her shirt and sprayed a woodsy winter fragrance around her throat.

The room filled with the heady aroma of tobacco and leather. Kathy loved it.

"Thanks for the warning... I think!" she added, slapping Helen playfully on the behind. "Come on, hero, let's go!"

***

Andrea was a fantastic cook, Kathy had to give her that. The dinner menu consisted of Dijon chicken casserole and dumplings served with honey-roasted carrots and parsnips, and they washed it down with an expensive Australian chardonnay. Kathy leaned back in the dining chair to relieve her full stomach.

Helen laughed, the corners of her eyes crinkling in the lamplight.

Circumstance
Kate Charlton

"Andrea, I think you've broken my girl!" She reached over and stroked Kathy's thigh tenderly. "You haven't even had dessert yet!"

David tilted his glass towards Kathy, his elbows resting on the edge of the table and his plate empty.

"I guess my darling sister didn't tell you that one of Andrea's favourite hobbies is feeding people. It takes time, but you learn that it's safer to treat dinner parties here like a marathon, not a sprint!" He threw back the remainder of his wine.

Andrea ignored the banter and rose majestically from the table with her reading glasses perched on her head.

"They say all of this, you know, but they never turn down a meal!" Her stern gaze darted between her husband and sister-in-law as she began to collect the finished plates.

Kathy saw a small smile playing at the corner of Andrea's lips and realised that deadpan was the woman's main form of humour. *I bet she can be bloody intimidating,* she thought as her gaze followed the slender woman around the kitchen.

David grinned as he topped up the wine glasses on the table.

Circumstance
Kate Charlton

"Her bark is far worse than her bite, I promise you," he whispered. His face held a sheen of perspiration, the only sign that the meal had beaten him, too.

Kathy blushed, realising that he had noticed her awed gaze, and hid it behind her wine glass.

The figure of an eight-year-old boy appeared in the kitchen doorway, dressed in superhero pyjamas, his shock of blonde hair standing up in all directions. Tentatively, he approached his aunt at the kitchen table.

"Hey, kiddo, what are you doing up and out of bed? It's getting late," Helen reminded him.

"Thomas Kennedy, what are you doing out of bed!" Andrea chastised, her hands planted firmly on her hips. It was the perfect annoyed mother stance.

"I couldn't sleep," he mumbled, his chin tucked down to his chest in his well-practised 'perfect, lovable child' look. "Will someone read to me?" he asked hopefully, his gaze falling on each of the grown-ups.

Kathy felt sorry for him, even though she knew she was probably being completely played by a small child. She stood, not giving herself the chance to weigh up the consequences from Andrea if she gave in.

Circumstance
Kate Charlton

"Come on, young man, I'll read you one chapter of something and then it's time for lights out, okay? You have school tomorrow, after all."

Thomas's face broke out into a grin.

"Thanks, Kathy!"

Andrea shook her head and patted Kathy gently on the shoulder.

"You've been reeled in hook, line, and sinker!" She shook her head teasingly.

Kathy couldn't decide whether it was intimidating or alluring. She mentally shook herself and followed the small boy to the staircase.

***

Meanwhile, Helen and Andrea sat out on the patio, wrapped up in their winter coats, whilst Helen smoked a cigarillo. The frost on the ground was already thick, blanketing everything in white. Moonlight caught the ice crystals on the grass. It shimmered like a million tiny diamonds. David had been tasked with preparing dessert while Kathy read to the young boy upstairs.

Andrea reached over and plucked the cigarillo from Helen's fingers. Gracefully, she slid it between her lips and inhaled deeply, rolling the smoke around her mouth and exhaling before handing it back.

"I've got to give it to you, Helen, she's pretty." Her voice was almost a whisper.

"Yes, she is, and she's all mine. I'm lucky."

Andrea twisted in her chair so she could see Helen better.

"Even with all of the shit she's got going on? It makes our murky past look like a comedy."

Helen shot her a warning glance that told Andrea to drop that line of conversation.

"Even with the shit."

"What about this accusation? What's happening with that?"

"She had a video conference meeting with her boss today to give her statement face-to-face. I don't think it took long, seeing as it never happened in the first place." She ran her thumb over the edge of her lighter, enjoying the weight of it in her palm. "I mean, come on, could you really see her as a sexual predator?"

Andrea shrugged. "I see all sorts of people in my line of work. You'd never think of them as monsters if you

Circumstance
Kate Charlton

saw them out on the street. I'm not saying that applies to Kathy!" she added hurriedly. "I'm saying it's very easy for people to make allegations these days, and mud sticks. It has to be investigated, but I'm sure it'll be over for her soon if there's nothing to answer for."

Helen loved her sister-in-law, but her black-and-white view of life sometimes riled her, even when she was right. She stubbed out her cigarillo, not wanting to dig any deeper into this line of conversation.

"Come on, let's go and have some dessert."

***

Kathy lay with her head on Helen's shoulder, her leg thrown over her lover's thighs and an arm draped leisurely over her belly. She loved this time of day, when it was just the two of them, safe under the duvet, cuddled up in the darkness and pretending that they didn't have a care in the world. She kissed Helen's warm shoulder and paused.

"You and Andrea have history, don't you? More than her just being married to David, I mean."

Helen looked down at the her, her blonde curls visible even in the darkness.

"A very long time ago. Sexual history more than relationship history, I'd say. Besides, once she met David, that was it. She was besotted with him and they've been blissfully happy ever since. There's certainly nothing sexual left between us anymore, if that's why you're asking."

Kathy squeezed her stomach reassuringly.

"No, that's not why I'm asking. I just noticed the way she looks at you sometimes. I don't think she even notices she's doing it, but there's a little glint of something for you. Did she break your heart when she picked David?"

"Oh, god, no. She and I had a bit of a fling, that was all. Besides, I met Meg shortly after that, so it was never an issue. Andrea's my sister-in-law, that's all. Don't be getting all jealous on me," she growled.

Kathy grazed her teeth over the place she'd just kissed on Helen's shoulder.

"I don't need to. I'd kill any woman who tried to steal you from me."

"Good."

They let the conversation trail off and lay contentedly together until they fell into a deep, peaceful sleep.

Circumstance
Kate Charlton

Chapter 20

In thick winter fog, vehicles crawled northbound up the A1 highway. Petra didn't mind, as it gave her the time to try to make sense of her thoughts. For some reason, she remembered Nigel—her first sexual partner. When she'd entered therapy at the age of fourteen, the psychiatrist was appalled that she was so nonchalant about it. She'd told Petra that, in the eyes of the law, Nigel had raped her. That was another reason she'd decided therapy wasn't for her—how could it be rape when she'd consented?

Her thoughts drifted back to when she'd first met him. He was one of her mother's 'friends', but he'd stuck around for a bit longer than the others. Before he came into their lives, her self-esteem was in the toilet. But Nigel... the moment he walked through the front door, he would always tell her how pretty she looked in her school uniform. It made her feel loved in a way she'd missed so much.

When her mother fell asleep, he'd stand on the landing just outside her bedroom. At only fourteen, her feelings for Nigel confused her. On one hand, she saw him as the father figure she'd lost. On the other, her teenage hormones were taking over. She knew what crushes were, but Nigel really captured her attention in a way no boys her age had.

She remembered Nigel standing by the window, smoking a cigarette. The only sound in the house was her mother's usual snore, until the toilet flushed at the end of the corridor. Petra froze in place, terrified her mother would come out and see the way she looked at him.

"*Go back to bed*," he told her finally. When she could move, she did as she was told—except, he followed her, clicking the door latch firmly in place behind him.

Stupid bitch, the voice inside her head taunted. *You're nothing but a stupid fucking bitch!* She turned the radio up higher to drown the voices out.

"Shut up, shut up, shut up!"

***

Alex Falsom sat in Madeline Rowe's impeccably decorated office, wondering what in the bloody hell was going on. He'd made the appointment to see her on Wednesday and he'd had to use all his charm to visit one of the biggest publishers in the city on such short notice.

She owned the company that published half the glamour magazines in the country.

Circumstance
Kate Charlton

She fixed her steely gaze on him and Alex shifted uncomfortably in his seat. He cleared his throat.

"You must know who this woman is, Ms. Rowe. You vet every damned employee in the company from the ground up."

She placed her hands flat on the desk before balling them into fists.

"I'm not telling you I don't know who she is, Mr. Falsom, I'm telling you that she doesn't exist, nor has she ever, within this company. Furthermore, my secretary remembers your employee well and has been able to provide a statement saying that the only people Miss Harland ever spoke to were the security staff on the main reception and herself when retrieved Miss Harland from the lobby." She closed the personnel files on the computer and straightened the collar of her baby-blue shirt. "I think you've probably been played and that this allegation is all bullshit, to put it politely. I suggest you get back in touch with the silly little girl who's playing these games and tell her you'll call the police if she doesn't cease and desist."

Alex slumped back in his chair, feeling like someone had knocked the air out of his lungs. Who in hell was the woman who'd fed him such a perfect and well-contrived lie earlier in the week? Not to mention wasted his time and valuable staff hours.

Circumstance
Kate Charlton

He thanked his host and strode from the office, pulling his tie away from his throat roughly. One thing he didn't appreciate was being played, and she'd done more than that. She'd trampled all over him as though it was his first week on the job. He wedged his mobile phone against his ear as he reached into his Italian leather briefcase for car keys.

He wanted Juliet Harker back in his office by the end of the day.

***

The doorbell rang, breaking Kathy's concentration as she prepared the ingredients for a chicken chasseur. She hurriedly wiped her hands on a tea towel and rushed down the hallway, her slippers swishing over the wood, then glanced through the peep-hole and saw a figure half-hidden behind a huge bouquet of flowers. She swung the door open.

The delivery guy peeked around the display.

"Kathy Harland?"

"That's me!" she acknowledged.

He thrust the flowers in her direction and hurried back to his van.

Circumstance
Kate Charlton

That's strange. Who sends a dozen black roses? Helen wasn't always the conventional type, but she'd never send these. She placed the display gently on the kitchen countertop and plucked the card from the centre of the blooms. The message was cryptic. No name, no kisses.

Wherever you are in life, always remember I'm with you.

Pulling her phone out of her pocket, she thumbed, *Beautiful roses, babe, but black, really? Lol. Never mind. I love them, anyway. Thank you.*

It was another half hour before Kathy's phone rang.

"Hey, babe. How are you? The flowers are certainly unusual, but they're beautiful nonetheless."

"Kathy, honey, I have no idea what you're talking about. I haven't sent you any flowers today, and if I had, why would I send you black roses?"

It was as if someone had knocked the air out of her lungs. She turned, her eyes falling on the sinister display.

"Are you sure? You haven't sent them and forgotten?"

"I'm certain. Isn't there a card?"

Her hands shook as she read the message to Helen.

"Admittedly strange, but check with Mike first to see if they're from him. He likes the weird, wonderful, and avant-garde."

Both women knew that it was an extremely unlikely scenario. Helen had to go because she had another patient waiting. Kathy instantly reached out to Michael and he, too, confirmed that the flowers weren't from him.

Fucking crazy bitch.

Reluctantly, she dialled the detective's number and listened to the dial tone ring in her ear. She didn't want to call him again, but it had to stop. Petra had to be stopped. Kathy's mind began to spin and she suddenly felt very alone in the big, empty house.

She rushed to the bathroom, cold sweat beading her face and her hand clamped to her mouth, and fell to her knees in front of the toilet, violently heaving.

From her pocket, her phone buzzed. On the cold tile floor, she lifted the phone to her ear.

"Hello," she said, her voice strained.

"Kathy," Alex said. "I've sorted a few things out." She listened as he relayed the story of the woman that had accused her. She'd said her name was Juliet Harker.

Circumstance
Kate Charlton

Kathy's stomach clenched, and she closed her eyes, hoping she wouldn't be sick again. *That bitch.*

"How did you know she wasn't who she said she was?" she asked him.

"I went to see Madeline Rowe at her office this morning to get some background and witness information regarding the complaint against you. I was left sitting with my dick in my hands, for want of a better phrase, when she told me that no such person had ever worked for her."

"Now what?"

"Obviously, the allegations against you have been proven false and malicious. It goes without saying that the suspension is lifted, however, I think you could do with the holiday with pay after this, so come back after Christmas."

"Thank you, Alex." She sighed. "Just email any case notes that I'll need for my return."

They said their goodbyes and wished each other a Merry Christmas. However, festivities and celebrations were yet again far from Kathy's mind.

***

Circumstance
Kate Charlton

Helen called to say she was working late, which meant she wouldn't be home until after seven. Every noise made Kathy jump. She shut herself in the living room with the curtains drawn, fire roaring, and TV on to try and make the room as comforting as possible. It was the only way she felt safe. When the house phone rang, she assumed it was Helen, informing her she was on her way home.

"Hello?" she said, cradling the phone against her ear.

There was a brief pause on the other end of the line before the caller responded.

"I see you got the flowers. I just thought that black roses would be perfect to mirror your black heart, darling." The woman's voice was low and cultured, her accent refined.

Kathy's face contorted in horror and she ripped the device away from her ear to check the caller display. *Unknown number. Fuck.* Reluctantly, she put it back.

"Petra, why are you doing this to me? Why can't you just leave me the fuck alone?!"

"You didn't learn, did you? You made damned sure that you ripped Anna from me, and for what? You didn't want her! You just didn't want to see her happy. You have to pay for that. And you will."

Circumstance
Kate Charlton

The line went dead, leaving Kathy staring at a black screen.

***

The moment Helen walked through the door, Kathy threw herself into her arms, almost knocking her over in the process, and convulsed into huge, wracking sobs.

"Come on, honey, calm down and talk to me. What's going on?"

Kathy tried to calm her breathing. "I'm sorry, darling, I haven't even let you get through the door."

"Hey, don't be sorry. I just want to know what's going on." She dropped her briefcase next to the coat rack and shrugged out of her jacket, her eyes never leaving Kathy's.

Wrapping her arms around herself, Kathy diverted her gaze to the ceiling.

"Petra rang me and asked if I liked the flowers. She said they matched my heart." She met Helen's gaze again. "Then she started rambling about how I'd torn Anna from her even though I didn't want her. She told me she's going to make me pay for it all, and then she hung up."

Helen found herself at a loss for words. She pulled Kathy back into her arms and held her for what felt like hours. The situation had escalated, and she was genuinely scared that one of them was going to end up dead.

***

David sat with legs spread wide as he cradled his mug of tea. He'd just finished the late shift at the station and had detoured to his sister's place on his way home.

"The only way either of you would be guaranteed safety is to have twenty-four-hour surveillance and the department doesn't have the manpower. My advice to both of you: leave the country until we catch her."

Kathy closed her eyes. "If she can find me here, what's to stop her from locating me in another country?"

He swirled the dregs of tea around in the bottom of his cup.

"Well, there are simple security measures you can take. Change your phone numbers, install security cameras, and never go anywhere alone–either of you."

Helen stood and hugged her body tightly. "Again, not exactly practical when we're both working. I mean, what the hell are the police actively doing to catch this woman? It's as though they aren't bothered anymore and she's become an invisible monster."

"I appreciate your frustration. I just don't have all the answers you're wanting to hear. We both know it's not that easy, sis." David shook his head sadly.

Nothing in life ever is, Helen thought. All she wanted to do was protect the woman she loved, yet she felt completely helpless. It was like trying to catch a ghost.

Circumstance
Kate Charlton

Circumstance
Kate Charlton

Chapter 21

The next morning, Helen walked beside Kathy along the bridge in Durham. Kathy leaned over the high ledge that over looked the River Wear as it meandered through the woodlands below. Up on the hillside to the left, a majestic castle watched over the city as it had for the past nine centuries—amazing that it still looked so new.

Helen wrapped her arm around Kathy's waist and followed her gaze up the hill.

"Incredible, isn't it?"

"It absolutely is. I bet it's magnificent inside, too," Kathy answered, kissing her lover on her cheek.

"Well, we can walk up there and take one of the tours if you like? We can visit the cathedral too, seeing as they're next to each other."

Kathy grinned. "I'd love that! Come on, let's do it." She grabbed Helen's gloved hand and pulled her away from the wall.

It was good to get out, even good to get away from Newcastle for a little while. The constant reminder that they weren't even safe in their own home had led to another sleepless night for both of them. Kathy's constant state of perpetual exhaustion had returned with a vengeance with Petra's reappearance and she worried about how much more of it Helen would be able to take, despite her constant reassurances that she wasn't planning to go anywhere. Refusing to let herself lapse back into a depression, Kathy forced the dark thoughts from her mind, determined that this was going to be a time for the two of them to be a couple and have a little fun.

As they reached the top of the hill, Kathy's breath caught in her throat as the square opened out in front of them to reveal the marketplace. Imposing, four-storey Victorian buildings loomed over the monuments of Neptune and the third Marquess of Londonderry. The spire of St. Nicholas church dominated the eastern side of the square, making her feel amazingly small as she stood still and took it all in.

"You're loving this, aren't you?" Helen pushed a lock of hair back from Kathy's forehead.

"I am. It's an incredible place. I could see myself coming back here; there's far too much to explore in a day."

"I suppose I take it for granted, really," Helen mused. "It's on my doorstep so I don't see it through someone else's eyes. You're right, though. It is breath-taking—as are you in that outfit!" She winked.

Letting out a rambunctious laugh, Kathy gave her a little push.

"Oh, come on! It's jeans and a grey polo-neck jumper! That is not *sexy,* Doc!"

"Yeah, but the way it clings to your curves definitely is."

Kathy pulled her close. "Come on, Romeo, feed your girl and then you can show me the castle and let me play princess for the afternoon."

"Your wish is my command, princess. Come on." Helen dropped her arm and grabbed Kathy's hand, their cool fingers lacing together in a perfect fit.

***

At the far end of the bridge, obscured by a statue, Petra took pictures of them with her Nikon camera. Each time the women showed affection, she felt nauseated. She would have that with Anna, but these bitches were in her way right now.

She pulled the black cable-knit hat lower down over her forehead and adjusted her mirror-lens sunglasses. It wasn't the most imaginative disguise, but paired with her new hairstyle, Petra felt reassured that Kathy could walk by and have no idea who she was. A small smile crossed her lips and she gave a pout. She suddenly felt much stronger.

***

"Thank you for taking me there, Helen. I can't wait to go back."

With her legs sprawled on the sofa, Kathy laid her head back, picturing the history and the far-off lands of Saint Cuthbert and Saint Bede. She'd laughed at the look on Helen's face as she dragged her around every accessible inch of the castle. She fell in love with the enormous portraits and tales of its grey lady ghost and marvelled at Saint Cuthbert's tomb and the majestic pointed arch ceilings in the nave vault.

"Can we can go back on our next weekend off?"

"I'd like that," Helen answered as she handed Kathy a glass of wine.

Kathy smiled and wiggled her toes against Helen's muscular thigh. "I'm really excited about getting the tree tomorrow!"

Circumstance
Kate Charlton

"I don't know why we can't just use the plastic one out of the loft. I'm sure I've got a few bits of tinsel up there to tart the place up, too."

"Hush your mouth, Scrooge. It's Christmas and we have friends and family descending upon us, and I'm not having a hunk of plastic as our decorative festive offering! As planned, we're going to the forest and finding the best damned tree they have!"

Groaning, Helen gulped down her wine and pinched Kathy's toes between her fingers. "They drop needles everywhere, Kathy!"

Kathy stuck out her bottom lip and strained to make her eyes water.

"But baby, it's our first Christmas together. Just imagine coming down on Christmas morning to the smell of pine and the sight of twinkling lights. If I get my real tree, I'll let you unwrap me every day from now until Christmas…" She licked her bottom lip seductively and grinned.

Helen blinked back and smiled.

"What size tree do you want, honey?"

Circumstance
Kate Charlton

Circumstance
Kate Charlton

Chapter 22

The image of Helen dressed in her grey cargo pants, navy check-flannelette shirt, and bright red padded body warmer left Kathy unable to keep a straight face. Helen stretched her arms above her head and stretched out her hamstrings by grabbing her heels one at a time and pulling them up to her behind.

"Helen, for god's sake, we're going to buy a Christmas tree, not entering into a wilderness survival expedition! What are you doing?"

Helen frowned while digging around her pocket.

"Hey, it's rugged terrain out there, you know! Where are my smokes?"

Kathy reached into her handbag and pulled out the square metal tin. "Here you go."

After plucking a cigarillo from the container, Helen rolled it between her fingers before lighting it. "Let's get going before I change my mind."

"No one told me when I met you on holiday that I was falling in love with a Grinch!" Kathy joked.

Circumstance
Kate Charlton

"What can I say, baby? Rough with the smooth and all that. Anyway, I'm stunningly gorgeous and I have a fabulous sense of humour. It would be unfair to the rest of mankind if I was blessed with a permanently cheery demeanour, too."

Kathy linked Helen's free arm. "So modest, too. Come on! My tree awaits."

They followed hordes of families into the forest and watched small children run and play while their parents looked for the right tree.

It reminded Kathy of when she was a child and her parents took her to pick out their Christmas tree from the local woods. They'd be out together in their old but sturdy Lada, deliberating over which tree would fit the big bay window perfectly that year. Her father would buy a big bag of cooked chestnuts to eat on the journey, filling the air with a woody, festive aroma. She remembered the battered old trapper hat that he'd insist on wearing, even though she refused to touch it because it was lined with real rabbit fur. Her mother tried to throw it away as winter approached, but he'd always manage to dig it out of the bin or stop her before she could get that far. She missed the time with her parents. She missed the family tradition that continued right up until she left home.

***

Circumstance
Kate Charlton

Kathy pointed towards a seven-foot noble fir that looked like the king of the forest.

"Honey, *this* is our tree!" she declared, clasping her hands in front of her chest.

Shoving her hands into the pockets of her body warmer, Helen grimaced as she rocked back on her heels and regarded the monster before her. She wondered how the hell they'd get something that size onto the roof rack and into her house.

"Babe, I think we may have to lower our expectations just a little bit here. It's enormous!"

Kathy raised her brow, her face stern and determined. "Helen, this isn't negotiable. I want that tree. We're having that tree, and now you're going to get your wallet out and go and pay the nice man to bundle it up in netting and strap it to the car."

"You're going to owe me for this one." She dug into the back pocket of her trousers to retrieve her old black leather wallet and ambled over to the guy wearing a knitted brown bobble hat.

***

They lay together on the sofa in front of a crackling fire and admired their handiwork. It'd taken them all day, but four fur-trimmed stockings hung from the Victorian oak mantle, and the tree, perfected with an ornate tree topper, glittered with string lights beneath vintage red and silver baubles.

Stroking her fingers through Kathy's curls, Helen murmured, "Are you happy with it all?"

Kathy pulled Helen's arm tightly around her waist. "It's absolutely perfect. Thank you for putting up with my Christmas-zilla behaviour. I just wanted our first one together to be really special."

"It will be, honey. I'll make sure of it."

***

The bed-and-breakfast room Petra was currently calling home was cosy, but impersonal. She sat, her head propped up by her arm, on the single bed next to the window and looked down on the busy road below. It wasn't long before she became hypnotised by the steady stream of cars and pedestrians. Heavy blue chintz curtains obscured part of her view, but she didn't care. All she could think about was the sense of overwhelming sadness that washed over her like a tidal wave. Hours went by, but she sat in the same position with her legs crossed in front of her, her fingers tugging at the duvet cover while she wondered how her life had gotten to this point.

Circumstance
Kate Charlton

Refusing to feel self-pity, she hauled herself up to sit on the side of her bed, and with a new determination, she crossed the room to the small wardrobe to see what clothes she had with her. Two pairs of faded denim jeans and a few shirts. She didn't need much. After she showered and applied make-up, she was going out.

She wouldn't be spending tonight alone.

...

The first bar she walked into was dimly lit and smelled faintly of blocked drains. Her nose wrinkled, but she threw her shoulders back confidently and strode across the wooden floor towards the bar, enjoying the glances she got from the women and even a few of the guys. Disco lights from the DJ booth in the corner reflected on the mirror and bottles behind the bar. Petra glanced at her reflection. *I look pretty hot tonight*, she mused as she waited for the young and very gay bloke to take her order.

"What can I get you, sweetie?" he shouted over the thumping bass line.

Leaning in closer, her gaze flitted briefly over the bottles of spirits. "Can you do me a Long Island Iced Tea?"

Circumstance
Kate Charlton

He looked at her dubiously and she realised that the only cocktails this place served were the kind that came in jugs and involved alcohol that tasted like a kid's drink.

Raising a perfectly tweezed eyebrow, he put a hand on his hip. "If you tell me what's in it, I can do it."

"Vodka, white rum, gin, tequila, and triple sec. A shot of each then a shot of lemon juice over ice. Fresh squeezed will do. Top it with coke."

With a click of his fingers, he spun around and gathered a large glass.

"And that will put you on your back, but hey, if you've got the money, I've got the skills!"

Petra smiled as she watched him concoct her drink, and once he was done, she handed him a ten and told him to keep the change. The kind gesture earned her a kiss blown across the bar. She took her drink, found a stool along the back wall, and glanced at the unfamiliar faces.

One group in particular caught her eye as she sipped her drink slowly through a black straw. There were five women, all older than her, maybe even late forties or early fifties. She had no idea if they were gay or straight, but she didn't care. When she set her mind to something, she got it. Petra's attention had been drawn to an older woman—tall, slim, nice muscle in all the right places, and

Circumstance
Kate Charlton

blonde wavy hair that cascaded over her shoulders the way Anna's did. She blinked several times as her eyes wandered over the muscular yet feminine backside beneath a white floral frock. She could imagine digging her nails into that.

With one large gulp, Petra emptied her glass and began pushing between the throng of customers, moving closer to where the object of her attention stood. She deliberately began to search through her bag, her eyes focused downward as she manoeuvred herself to the left so she'd bump into the woman's side. As planned, she ran into the woman hard enough to knock her drink to the floor.

"Jesus, I'm so sorry! I'm such a klutz. That was careless of me. Please, let me replace that for you, it's the least I can do. Anyone else's, too, if I've spilled theirs." Her gaze flickered around the group.

"I think it was just mine you got. Vodka and diet coke, thanks."

Petra turned to the bar.

"Two more of the same." She held a twenty between her fingers and passed it to him.

The drinks came back and she handed one to her new friend.

Circumstance
Kate Charlton

"This isn't vodka and coke," the blonde remarked.

Petra leaned in and breathed in the scent of shampoo as she brushed a fingertip across the woman's hand. "I felt bad, so I thought I'd give your order an upgrade."

"Very fucking sure of yourself, aren't you?" The woman narrowed her gaze, but the words held a tone of teasing instead of anger.

"What can I say? When I see a woman I want, I go for it."

Sipping her drink, the woman mirrored her and gave a full grin. "How do you know I'm gay and how do you know that one of these women isn't my girlfriend?"

"I don't know the answer to either, but I'd never have found out and always would have wondered if I hadn't spilled your drink."

"Take me out for a cigarette and maybe I'll give you the answers you're looking for," the woman said.

They stood outside the bar, huddled close to keep warm.

"So, what's your name?"

"Petra. Yours?"

Circumstance
Kate Charlton

"Diane. I'm fifty-four, I'm bi, and I'm single. You don't need my life history. I don't suppose you're looking for a long-term relationship and a happily-ever-after, right?" The lines around Diane's eyes and mouth were evident as she spoke.

Seductively, Petra raised an eyebrow. "What makes you say that?"

"You're a young woman drinking in a gay bar all by your lonesome and you don't sound like you're from around here. My powers of deduction tell me you're from out of town and you're looking for someone to get your rocks off."

This time, it was Petra who grinned. "I like a woman who's straight-forward."

Diane stubbed her cigarette out with the heel of her shoe. "We haven't been out long. Have a few drinks with us and then we can go back to wherever it is you're staying. You don't keep an axe and a few bodies under your bed, do you?"

"Not yet," Petra muttered.

***

They sat in the back of a black cab, facing away from the driver as he maneuvered through the bustling city streets. Diane's short dress had ridden up high enough that her white underwear would have been visible to anyone sitting opposite. Petra reached across and slipped her hand into the skimpy knickers, eliciting a gasp and a giggle from her companion. She didn't give a shit whether the driver could hear them or not. She let her index finger trail up and down the smooth, engorged flesh and grinned at the wetness that coated her finger. She then removed her hand and brought her finger to her mouth, removing the slick juices with her tongue.

The driver waved off the two lovers as the door slammed closed behind them. They tumbled into the room, a tangle of arms and legs, and kissed hungrily. Petra stripped Diane out of her dress in seconds and yanked her bra down, cupping one breast tightly as she sucked the other into her mouth. She wasn't looking to make love. She wanted hot, raw sex, and that was exactly what she intended to get.

"You like treating your women rough, do you?" Diane asked huskily.

Petra paused for a moment to meet her gaze. "Sometimes."

Her voice was devoid of all emotion apart from one: need. She pushed Diane back, onto the bed, and slid on top of her, her mouth exploring the soft, warm skin and ripples of muscle beneath. She licked, sucked, and bit her way down from throat to chest, chest to breasts, breasts to belly.

Giggling, Diane grabbed Petra's chin in her fingers. "Come on then, what are you waiting for? Fuck me."

Two fingers ploughed into Diane's wet centre and curled forward, eliciting a gasp from the helpless woman on the bed.

"I intend to." Petra felt powerful again, knowing that this stranger was letting her fuck her in any way she chose. She pulled an erect nipple hard, then pushed a third finger inside.

"Who do you screw most, men or women?" she growled.

Throwing her head back against the pillows, Diane's mouth formed an O as she let herself be used.

"Both. My last relationship was with a guy," she ground out.

The sight of slick flesh around her fingers, fingers that were now coated in this woman's juices, made Petra crave more.

"Did you let him fuck you like this?"

"N-no…" she stuttered.

Stretching her even wider, Petra pushed until all five fingers were working their way inside. Satisfied that Diane could take it, she thrust deep into the wet pussy. Diane screamed out as Petra's mouth descended onto her breast, licking and biting while her hand fucked deeper and harder.

Petra lost all sense of her surroundings as she roughly took the woman beneath her. Their bodies, slick with sweat, were a tangle of limbs in the twisted sheets. She was completely unaware that she was still fully clothed until she felt Diane's fingers fumbling to remove her jeans. She spread her legs as wide as she could, letting this Diane finger-fuck her just as hard in return. The sensations of pleasure and pain pushed out the screaming noises and voices in her head, just long enough to let the roaring orgasm wash over her. For a wonderful moment, she could think of nothing but the pulsating ache between her legs. She pushed her fist into Diane once more, feeling the woman's powerful orgasm match her own.

Finally, they collapsed together, both exhausted from alcohol and sex. Petra rested her head on Diane's shoulder and laid an arm around her middle, cuddling into her body as though they were lovers who had been together forever. In her mind, the woman who held her back was Anna, her beautiful Anna who made her world okay again.

Circumstance
Kate Charlton

Circumstance
Kate Charlton

Chapter 23

A large brown envelope laid flat at the foot of the door. Helen noticed it as she galloped down the stairs, holding her empty water glass in one hand and Kathy's coffee mug in the other. She paused on the bottom step and frowned at the ominous-looking parcel.

"Darling, did you hear anyone at the door last night?" she called back up to Kathy.

Appearing at the top of the staircase in her dressing gown and slippers, Kathy leaned over the rail and gave Helen a curious look.

"No, why?"

"We have a delivery," she mumbled as she swept the envelope up from the carpet.

Both headed for the kitchen as morning coffee became their focus. Helen took a heavy, thin-bladed knife from the stainless-steel block and carefully cut along the crease at the top whilst Kathy looked over her shoulder. Gently, she lifted it by a bottom corner and shook out the contents. They stood there for a moment and peered at the images through narrowed eyes.

Circumstance
Kate Charlton

Kathy gasped, "It's photographs of us. That bitch has been following us! Look: Durham, the forest the other day. She's been there and we had no idea." She reeled back and stared at the photos.

With an involuntary shudder, Helen carefully picked each photo up by the corner and laid them out on the bench. "She's playing with us. This is her way of telling us that she can get to us at any time."

The tableau of images showed them on the bridge in Durham as they kissed, pictures of them eating lunch in a small pub in the city, and a close-up shot of them in the car. Helen's gaze roamed to the next set of pictures of them in the woods, hand-in-hand. She clenched her fists by her sides and her nostrils flared. Petra had followed them everywhere.

"How the hell didn't we see her? It's not as though we're not on guard twenty-four-fucking-seven." Kathy pushed the curls out of her eyes, her jaw set rigidly as she stood glowering at the images in front of her.

"She's escalating, Kathy, and there's no way you're staying home alone today."

"Don't be ridiculous! We've got Michael and Paul arriving tomorrow and I have a lot to do before they get here. Besides, where am I going to go?"

"To work, with me," Helen replied.

Wagging her finger at her lover's face, Kathy's dressing gown fell open slightly across her breasts. "No way. No. What the hell would I do all day? Sit in an empty consulting room and read a book or prepare depositions?"

Helen said nothing.

"Helen Kennedy, there's no way in hell I'm doing that. I'm staying right here in this house and I am not going to let that bitch win." Her eyes flashed as her voice rose.

Digging her hands into the pocket of her pyjama bottoms, Helen huffed loudly.

"Fine," she growled. She pulled her phone out of her pocket and slapped it against her ear. "Morning, Andrea. Sorry to call so early. What are you doing today?"

Kathy's mouth fell open and she threw her arms up in the air and stormed out of the kitchen, her slippers slapping against the wooden floor.

**

Shaking the freshly-laundered sheet out over the double guest bed, Kathy kept her mouth shut, but her head buzzed with rage. Her lips were a thin line. She'd barely spoken since Andrea arrived. Her temporary babysitter, as she viewed her, caught the other side of the sheet and together, they stretched it out and tucked it in.

Andrea stretched the crick from her back and glared at Kathy with her hands firmly on her hips.

"I get it. You're pissed off that you've got a babysitter. But thundering around the house like an angry water buffalo is not the way to make it better!"

Kathy stopped. Her mouth worked as she searched for a response, but finally she covered her face with her hands and burst into a fit of giggles. "A water buffalo? Really?"

"Yes!" Andrea's eyes remained narrowed as she studied her charge.

"I know you're right, and I know you probably had plenty to do today. God knows I do and I haven't even got kids. I'm sorry for being a bitch." Kathy flopped down onto the bed. "What do you suggest?"

Andrea squinted as she tried to read the small hands on her watch.

"Well, it's eleven-thirty. By the time we get the metro into town, it'll be lunchtime and I think it's perfectly acceptable for us to have champagne lunch. What do you say?"

Circumstance
Kate Charlton

Waving her arms in the air, Kathy grinned. "Let's do it! Helen won't be home until at least six, and Michael and Paul's train won't get in until nearer nine. No reason to sit here and brood all day."

***

The booze-fuelled lunch passed in a blur of laughter and admissions. The women learned more about each other in an hour than they had in the past couple of months. Kathy felt extremely lucky that the whole family had accepted her despite all the baggage she'd dragged into Helen's life. A bottle of champagne turned into two before they spilled out of the restaurant and decided that a cab would be a far better option than trying to navigate their way on the metro.

***

They rolled into the house a little after five and headed straight for the kitchen. Andrea pulled herself up onto a barstool as Kathy deftly moved about and poured grounds of coffee into the pot as the kettle boiled.

"Were you ever in love with Helen?" Kathy asked.

Andrea folded her arms across her chest. Some of the cheer had gone out of her face.

Circumstance
Kate Charlton

"In love?" She gave a small, brittle laugh that lacked humour. "Was my marriage to David the end of our physical relationship? No."

Kathy spun around with the coffee scoop still in her hand.

"What do you mean?"

"Shit," Andrea muttered, pulling a piece of lint from her jeans.

Kathy strode across the kitchen and stood in front of her. "Come on, Andrea, tell me."

Groaning, Andrea threw her head back dramatically. "Ah, Kathy, it doesn't matter anymore."

Kathy grabbed her hand and squeezed. "Yes, it does. To me it does."

Andrea entwined her fingers with Kathy's and held them tightly. "When I got pregnant with Hannah, David and I had broken up—a glitch in the marriage, so to speak. We'd been having a hell of a rough time: we were going through IVF, he'd just been promoted at work, and the stress was too much, so he rented a flat for a while. We were still intimate. I became pregnant—quite by chance since I never thought it could happen without help, but it did."

Circumstance
Kate Charlton

A sad smile crossed her lips as her gaze went past Kathy towards the window. Her eyes were distant, as if she was drifting through her memories. "I lost my shit, to put it politely. I had no clue if David and I were going to make it, I didn't know if I wanted the baby or if I was going to be a single parent…" She paused to collect her thoughts and ran her thumb over the back of Kathy's hand. "I rang Helen. I didn't know who else to call. She's so like David but so different at the same time. So she came over and Meg stayed at home, quite happy to let her wife come to the rescue, and I was happy to have her there."

"Go on," Kathy urged.

"She came over, armed with a pizza and a four-pack of diet cola; she knew how to show a woman a good time." She laughed lightly. "I cried and told her about everything that'd gone on: how David and I rowed every day, how I dreaded him coming home, and how terrified I was that I found myself pregnant and facing a divorce."

Kathy pushed her free hand deeply into her trouser pocket. "Who made the first move?"

Circumstance
Kate Charlton

Andrea met her gaze for the first time during the whole conversation. Andrea's tough, no-nonsense mask had finally slipped and a vulnerable woman with a wealth of emotions broke free.

"I'd cuddled up to her after crying myself half to death. We were watching a film and I was exhausted and starting to nod off until she kissed the top of my head and told me it was time for me to go to bed. I was so scared of being alone, so without thinking, I kissed her—and she kissed me back. The next thing I knew, she picked me up and carried me to bed like something out of a Brontë novel."

Andrea released Kathy's hand and hopped off the stool. She paced the kitchen, her hands laced behind her head. A muscle at the side of her mouth twitched as she stood and looked beyond Kathy. Her expression was resigned.

"How long did the affair last?" Kathy asked gently.

"Four-and-a-half years," she whispered as her gaze met the floor. Tears tumbled down Andrea's cheeks and she covered her face as heaving sobs wracked her body.

Circumstance
Kate Charlton

Kathy strode across the kitchen and took Andrea in her arms.

"She ended it when Meg was diagnosed, didn't she?"

Sniffing loudly, Andrea nodded and clung to her, tears dripping onto Kathy's shirt.

Circumstance
Kate Charlton

Circumstance
Kate Charlton

Chapter 24

The moment they arrived back at the house, Helen and David could hear the girls chatting in the kitchen as they made their way through the hallway. The siblings laughed at their slightly intoxicated spouses as the women regaled them with the tale of their drunken afternoon in an upmarket restaurant. They made themselves comfortable as they drank hot coffee and opened a box of mince pies. Kathy and Andrea had shot each other a look that spoke a thousand words as Helen and David chatted. The gentle look between them sealed a secret that would never be spoken of to their significant others.

Even though Kathy knew it was over between Helen and Andrea, she still felt on edge, and watched closely for any surreptitious looks from Helen to reveal any residual feelings for her sister-in-law.

So many questions swam around in her head, but she knew that it wouldn't be Helen who could answer them. She felt as though her whole world was off-balance as soon as she thought she'd found her feet.

***

Circumstance
Kate Charlton

Michael and Paul bounded from the train as though they were jumping off a page from a luxury men's fashion magazine. Michael, dressed as immaculately as ever in a knee-length black wool coat, grey marl jumper, and skinny black trousers, approached Kathy with arms open wide as Paul pulled a large aluminium designer suitcase behind him.

Kathy leaned into Michael's arms and allowed her tears to flow.

"I've missed you so much," Helen heard her whisper into Michael's collar.

Michael swept her off her feet and twirled her around, laughing as she squealed and clung to his neck.

"Put me down, you big idiot!" she giggled.

They linked arms and chatted as Helen and Paul followed close behind. Helen loved seeing her so happy and so animated; it was the spark that Kathy had lacked since she'd arrived on her doorstep a week and a half ago. It saddened her that her lover seemed so alive only when a little piece of home appeared. Kathy was not the same when they were in Newcastle as she was in London. She shrugged the nagging feeling off as they passed through the enormous wooden doors that led out of the taxi rank and into the bitingly cold Northern air.

Circumstance
Kate Charlton

***

Conflicting emotions and thoughts swamped Kathy's mind after learning of Helen and Andrea's secret affair. The fact that it only ended after Meg was diagnosed made her wonder if the relationship would have continued if things had been different and why they hadn't continued the relationship after Meg's death. She knew that Helen wasn't obliged to give her any information about her past, but when it was something so fucking big and so significant, and the fact that after admitting they had an affair, she lied about when it ended…

She sprawled on the sofa and stared into the orange flames of the flickering fireplace as the silver smoke curled up the chimney breast. She was trying to fight away the thoughts of Helen and Andrea in each other's arms. Michael made himself quite at home as he sat on the carpet in front of the armchair, savouring a glass of cognac, and Paul retired early to bed with a migraine.

"What's going on with you?" Concern filled Michael's eyes. He swirled the amber liquid around in the glass and inhaled the spicy aroma.

"Do you think a relationship can make it if one partner keeps a huge secret?" she blurted, swinging her legs around so that she now sat on the edge of the sofa where she could see him properly.

"It depends on the secret," he replied, shrugging his shoulders as he crossed his legs.

With a deep sigh, she stared back into the flames and sipped her tea, her lips curving into a bitter smile. "I ended up going for lunch with Helen's sister-in-law today. I knew they had a past; Helen told me they dated for a couple of weeks before Andrea met her brother."

"But?" Michael encouraged her.

She was exhausted. Her limbs ached from a chill she couldn't shake, no matter how warm the room was. She wanted to go to bed and hibernate.

"But… that wasn't the end of it, which was what Helen had led me to believe. It turns out that David and Andrea were going through a rough patch when they were trying to conceive. David moved out for a while and Andrea turned to Helen for support, but it went further than that. They had an affair."

"Okay." He paused. "Maybe she chose to keep it quiet because it's her sister-in-law, after all. People make mistakes; they don't always choose to talk about them, though."

Cupping her chin in her hand, she gave a small smile that failed to reach her eyes.

Circumstance
Kate Charlton

"A mistake is a few months, a year tops, Mikey. When it lasts for four-and-a-half years and only ends because Helen's wife was dying..." Her voice trailed off as she fought to keep her emotions in check. Her chest felt heavy, as though someone was sitting on her and squeezing the air out of her lungs. She inhaled deeply, trying unsuccessfully to shift the discomfort.

Shaking his head, pausing after each word, Michael murmured, "Shit, Kathy."

***

Petra eyed the bookcase in the corner of the room, her eyes narrowing on the titles. Keats, Woolf and King, the odd anthology of lesbian shorts, and lesbian romance. Her gaze wandered to the pictures on the mantelpiece. She retrieved a photo of a young man. She stroked the silver frame with her thumb, examining every detail.

"That's my son." Diane's voice made her jump as she placed the picture down with a clatter.

With a grin, Diane picked the frame back up and studied the image, her gaze becoming soft and tender.

"I don't mind you looking; you don't have to be so nervous. Cam is twenty-five and he lives with his girlfriend in Carlisle. Sit down, please."

Circumstance
Kate Charlton

Petra wandered over to the overstuffed cream sofa and settled into a corner. She crossed one leg over the other and gave Diane an appraising look, desire rising inside her when her gaze settled on the firm, pert breasts under the white tank top.

"I have to ask. How did you find me?" Diane asked. She settled into the opposite end of the sofa, her leg kicked underneath her.

"A business card had fallen out of your bag when you left the other night, so I took a chance and thought I'd try my luck a second time." She took a long drink from her bottle of beer, her eyes never leaving Diane's. She reminded her so much of Anna: the golden blonde hair, the slight imperfection in the set of her teeth, the lopsided smile that was as close to a come-on as a woman could give. She couldn't possibly tell her the truth and admit that she'd gone through her bag to find out who she was and how to contact her, or that she'd searched her social media sites to get more information on her.

It turned out that Diane was an event organiser, and a reasonably well-known one in the area, too. Her internet pages listed everything from charity galas to footballers' birthday parties and special invite occasions at some of the most well-known castles in Northumberland.

"Did you mind that I called you?" Petra asked coyly.

Circumstance
Kate Charlton

Diane reached out and stroked her arm. "I like to live on the edge from time to time. A sexy stranger taking me home from a club and fucking my brains out is one thing. When she enjoys it so much that she tracks me down for an action replay, how could my ego ever say no?" She winked.

Peta waved her hand towards the other room. She said nothing when Diane raised her brow and laughed. "How about we pick up where we left off?"

She followed close behind, her hands resting on Diane's hips as they walked through the house into the last room on the right.

***

Diane rested on the bed on her hands and knees, wrists bound to the headboard with a pink silk scarf. Her perfectly round behind stuck up in the air as deep, guttural moans escaped her lips. Petra slid a long, thin vibrator over her wetness, pushing the tip hard against her engorged clit, and knelt behind her, a strap-on snug against her own aching flesh. She wanted the woman in front of her so badly, but at the same time, she wanted the pleasure and torment to last as long as possible.

"Just how much can you take?" she drawled into Diane's ear.

Circumstance
Kate Charlton

"As much as you can give me," came the breathless reply.

When Diane had revealed a box under the bed that held enough toys to stock an adult store, Petra had been mesmerised. She'd pulled out a short leather crop, her eyes glinting in the dim lamplight as Diane gave her a cocky grin of approval.

Petra reached behind her and picked the crop up from the end of the bed. Pulling Diane's ass into the air, she reared back and brought the stiff leather down on the perfect creamy skin in front of her. Diane fell forward into the pillow, a scream leaving her perfect bow-shaped lips. Elation washed over Petra like a flood at the response her actions had created; this woman was hers and she'd do anything she liked to her, knowing that Diane would take anything she was given.

***

As Diane slammed the strap-on into her, Petra's body bucked hard. Her ankles were being held over her lover's shoulders, keeping her from moving and making her feel weightless as she lay there so helplessly, allowing her body to be used in a way that she'd never let a woman use her before. The submission made her feel strangely powerful as the throbbing between her legs grew with every second that passed; she felt wanted and needed in a way that she hadn't for a very long time. A wave of euphoria built inside her, pleasure and pain exploding into a crescendo of ecstasy that she'd craved for so long.

Diane pulled back and scrambled up the bed, her head resting against the headboard as she dragged Petra onto her lap.

Petra willingly impaled herself again as Diane's hungry mouth bit down on a swollen nipple. All at once, her orgasm erupted from the depths of her being as she threw her head back and roared. Tears coursed down her cheeks as the dam of raw emotion broke; there was nothing she could do to stop them.

Tenderly, Diane took her into her arms. Diane rocked her until she could cry no more. She'd lost all self-control. For the first time that she could remember, it hadn't resulted in anyone else getting hurt.

***

Lying on her back in the darkness, Kathy stared at the ceiling while she waited for Helen to finish her nightly bathroom routine. No matter how much she tried, she just couldn't get the thought of Helen and Andrea out of her mind and felt both angry and hurt that she'd had to find out from "the other woman".

Circumstance
Kate Charlton

Padding into the bedroom, Helen gently closed the door behind her, ensuring it wouldn't slam, removed her dressing gown, and hung it on the back of the door. She felt her way to her side of the bed, her silhouette visible against the weak light that filtered through the curtains as she stripped out of her pyjamas and slid beneath the duvet. She rolled towards Kathy and eased an arm over her bare stomach.

"Are you okay, honey?" she asked sleepily.

Without responding, Kathy took Helen's hand in her own, guided her fingers to her centre, and pushed them against her aching clit. Only a couple of hours ago, she'd been wondering if she should cut her losses, pack her things, and insist to Michael and Paul that they go home.

Helen groaned loudly. "Oh, baby, you feel good."

She nuzzled her face close to Kathy's neck.

"I don't want gentle. I don't want to make love. I want to be fucked. Hard. I want you to take control of me and fuck me senseless."

Helen's breath caught in her throat and she squeezed Kathy's clit.

Kathy's belly tensed and her mind raced with arousal.

***

Circumstance
Kate Charlton

Kathy's eyes were closed tightly as she knelt on the bed with Helen positioned behind her. Helen's left arm held her still, her grip firm across her torso. She sucked the soft flesh of Kathy's throat as her free hand rubbed and pulled her clit, slapping it forcefully when Kathy dared moan or gasp.

The pleasure and pain building between her thighs made her lose herself, turned on beyond belief at this wild side of Helen that she was seeing for the first time.

Did she fuck Andrea like this? She couldn't believe the thought turned her on as she was being taken. She growled with pleasure as her lips were pulled wide and two fingers entered her hot, wet pussy. Helen covered her mouth with her other hand to prevent her from waking their guests.

***

Helen was completely swallowed up by Kathy's desire and need. A sheen of perspiration covered her flesh and she pushed her down face first onto the bed. She pushed two fingers back inside her lover from behind, loving how the slickness that covered them drove her crazy and fuelled her own hunger.

She pulled her up and marched her over to stand in front of the full-length, mirrored-wardrobe door. She held

Circumstance
Kate Charlton

Kathy's chin between her fingers, forcing her to watch as she took her from behind with a strap-on toy. Her eyes glittered like shards of ice in the reflected moonlight. They each watched the other's reflection, both women past the point of sensibility. Kathy rubbed her clit hard as Helen's hands cupped her breasts, her fingers pulling at large, aching nipples.

"Fuck me!" she growled.

With her face buried in Kathy's shoulder, Helen fucked her harder, driven crazy by the moans that escaped her lover's lips. Their skin was slick with perspiration as she dragged her nails across Kathy's tight belly and, thrusting hard for one final time, allowed her own orgasm to explode from deep inside her. Kathy came at the same time, her legs buckling under her as exhaustion took over.

***

They collapsed together onto the carpet at the side of the bed, and Kathy allowed herself to be held close as silent tears ran down her cheeks. The orgasm had left her brain numb enough to dull her pain but not numb enough to forget. She could feel the rise and fall of Helen's full breasts against her back and squeezed her eyes tightly, trying to stop the tears from turning into wracking sobs that threatened to erupt.

Circumstance
Kate Charlton

Chapter 25

At the entrance of the café, Kathy ran her fingers through her hair and paused. She mentally agonised over going in and joining Andrea for lunch. She'd tried so hard to be understanding, but each time her thoughts returned to images of Helen making love to her. Andrea was already seated at the back of the café under the enormous wooden clock. *I can't keep avoiding her*. Her stomach flip-flopped as she made her way down the row of empty tables. Her rubber-soled boots squeaked on the polished wooden floor.

Half-smiling, Andrea glanced down at her watch. "You're late."

"I know, I got stuck in traffic. Have you been waiting long?"

"Not too long." Andrea's lips curved. "You look like shit."

"Thanks a lot." Kathy half-smiled. "It's hard to rest when you have a crazy stalker trying to ruin and your life. It doesn't help to learn the woman you share your bed with cheated on her last partner for four years." Kathy covered her mouth with her hand, but it was too late. For some reason, she couldn't guard her words around Andrea.

"I probably should've kept my mouth shut," Andrea said simply, her gaze lowered to the table top.

It was the first time Kathy had seen her mask of bravado slip. "In a way, I'm glad you told me. Yes, it's affected the perception I have of Helen and our relationship, but at the same time, I'm glad I've found out now, instead of down the road."

"You're not going to leave Helen over this, are you?" Andrea took a deep breath, a slight tremor shaking her mouth.

The heated gaze only lasted for a second. Kathy inhaled sharply and let it out just as fast.

"I love her, Andrea, but I don't know if I can do this." Kathy leaned forward, and whispered, "I'm hurt and disappointed that she hasn't told me about it. It's a hell of a big secret to keep from the woman you profess to love, don't you think?"

"Kathy, Helen's never loved me. She loves you. Losing Meg completely changed her in a way I can't describe, because you didn't know her then. She genuinely loved her too and she went through hell every time the doctor told them that the cancer had come back." She paused as the waitress asked to take their order.

Kathy was no longer hungry. She idly stirred a brown sugar cube into her cup and watched the dark liquid swirl around the spoon.

"You can't have an affair with someone for that long and not be in love with them. You can spit excuses at me all afternoon, but you can't deny that fact." She gave a harsh laugh. "We had sex the other night, and as she was inside me, I wondered if she'd fucked you the same way." She could feel the anger build, and she was afraid she'd reach over the table and slap Andrea. Instead, she gripped the seat of her chair until her knuckles turned white.

"Yes, I was in love with her." Andrea took a deep breath and rubbed her forehead with the heel of her hand. "I didn't know who I was when I was twenty. I was a selfish little brat who thought she knew everything there was to know about the world and I went out and got whatever I wanted. I knew I wanted a career in social work and I knew that I wanted to have a good life, a couple of kids, a secure relationship, but... But I knew that I'd have to lie to get that because I knew I was gay."

Kathy blinked several times. The awkward silence was broken when the waitress returned with their sandwiches.

"Did you love Helen before you met David?"

With a snort of mockery, Andrea took a deep breath. "I'd only known her a few weeks. But the stupid, young version of me thought that David would be the more appropriate choice for my life plan. I knew I loved her by the time I married him three years later."

"What happened then?"

"We were both having relationship issues. In Helen's case, she and Meg never saw one another because they both worked all the time."

Looking past Andrea's shoulder, Kathy noticed that a heavy snow had begun to fall outside. She smiled, despite her mood and simmering anger.

"Look. Isn't that beautiful?"

The view beyond the window was of a bleak, brick-walled alley, complete with rubbish bins, but the snowfall that clung to the bare tree beyond it made it somehow magical.

When Andrea turned her head, Kathy took in her profile. She could see why Helen found her attractive.

"Did you ever talk about leaving your partners for each other?" Kathy asked, a little less harshly than before.

"Once," she admitted. "Like I said, it ended when Meg was diagnosed."

Kathy found it hard to put everything into place. If only Andrea hadn't become pregnant, *click*. If only Meg had gone to the house with her that night, *click*. The combinations that had brought them together were only reversed by a life-threatening illness. *Would they have continued if Meg hadn't become sick? Would they be together now?* Sucking her bottom lip between her teeth, Kathy tried to fight the sting of tears that burned her eyes. That heavy lead weight had taken root in her chest again. *Why hadn't they resumed their relationship after Meg's death?*

She felt the words spill out of her mouth before she could think of the consequences that would surely accompany the reply.

Andrea blinked and took a sip of the rapidly cooling coffee. She paused for a few seconds, regarding Kathy over the rim.

"Like I've said before, losing Meg changed Helen immensely and she was never the same person after her death. I think she carried an awful lot of guilt about the affair and it would never have been right between us. She saw Meg's death as her penance for what she'd done to her for so long. I'm not saying she's ever said that, but I know Helen—our relationship was too tainted by everything that had happened to ever work in the real world. It was for the best, it's in the past, and that's where it's best left, for everyone's sake."

Kathy flexed her jaw as she mulled over the response. *Do they still love each other?* Would she spend the rest of their lives together wondering if the affair had started again behind her back? Could she trust either of them? Would she forever wonder if Helen did the same things in bed to her as she'd done to Andrea? Her head buzzed as the questions spun around in her mind until it was a roar in her ears. It was all too much.

"It's the past," Andrea said again as she placed her palms flat on the table. "Leave it there, Kathy. Whatever we once had, it has no impact on your current or future relationship. I was fucking stupid for saying anything in the first place."

Andrea looked agonised and tired, as though a thousand sins had come back to haunt her all at once. The stress of it seemed to age her instantly, and she looked drawn. Kathy reached across the table and took Andrea's cool hand in her own, stroking her thumb over the back of the smooth skin. She didn't speak. She had nothing more to add. Any decision she made now had to be about her and Helen's relationship,

Circumstance
Kate Charlton

***

From the table close to the door, Petra sat reading a broadsheet newspaper and intermittently checking her smartphone. The plain, thick-rimmed spectacles covered enough of her eyes and cheekbones to keep her identity hidden.

They may not have recognised her, but she certainly recognised Kathy, who was engaged in an intense and apparently emotional discussion.

Perfect timing. Petra snapped several photographs. *Surely the bitch isn't running around on her new lover already?* The emotional display had her curiosity heightened, and when they reached for each other's hands and tears streamed down their cheeks, Petra purposely made her way to the back towards the restroom. Once out of view, she leaned against the wall and listened.

She smiled to herself, scraping the sole of her boot over the wooden flooring. *Maybe this will be a very merry Christmas after all.* She allowed herself to enjoy the butterfly sensation as it grew in her belly as she inched closer without being seen.

"Can I get you something, ma'am?"

Petra's head snapped to the side.

Circumstance
Kate Charlton

"No…I'm waiting to go to the toilet." Her quick response must have satisfied the young woman because she smiled and hurried off.

Circumstance
Kate Charlton

Chapter 26

The worn leather armchair felt like someone wrapping their arms around Helen as she eased into it. She stared into the twinkling lights of the tree and sipped on the hot mug of black coffee, enjoying the warmth of the freshly-lit fire. The aroma of the beech logs filled her nostrils, bringing a smile to her lips. It reminded her of when she and Meg first found the festive wood while on holiday. She knew it wouldn't be long before Kathy woke to the glorious aroma, and she'd be forced to celebrate Christmas. She would never admit it to Kathy, but since they'd met, she marvelled at how she looked forward to sharing the holiday with her.

The year prior, she'd refused to celebrate Christmas, choosing self-pity and being locked in her house, the curtains drawn while losing herself in a bottle of whisky and Meg's photo albums—the only piece of Meg she had left.

She must have passed out, because when she had opened her eyes, Andrea and David stood in the doorway to the living room, holding a plate of cold, foil-wrapped Christmas dinner, and found her sprawled on the sofa, intoxicated and incoherent.

Circumstance
Kate Charlton

A feeling of shame and embarrassment had washed over her as Andrea stood over her. In that moment, she wished she'd died instead of her beautiful, innocent Meg, whom she'd spent years betraying.

Helen closed her eyes and cried. Since that day, the memories had faded, but the pain still resided in her chest.

Can you ever forgive me, Meg? She drank down the cold dregs of coffee, reminding herself that the past was the past and she had a chance to start over.

The peaceful stillness was interrupted by the letterbox rattling, then something heavy thudding onto the mat. From the window, she strained her eyes as she looked around the dark garden. The only thing in view was the blanket of snow that covered the earth. Despite the roaring fire and the beauty of the winter tableau, a cold shiver ran through her, making her pull her warm robe tight around her.

In the hallway, a large brown envelope lay on the floor. She picked it up. Scrawled across the front was *Doctor Helen Kennedy* in black marker.

It was obvious who'd sent it. It was identical to the one they'd received before. She had two choices. One was to wake Kathy and ruin her Christmas morning. Two was to open the damn thing, spill its contents, and decide whether or not to show it to her. Finally, she sat at the breakfast island and gently cut through the envelope seam with a small, sharp paring knife. Her stomach knotted with tension as the logical side of her brain warned not to disturb the package. It was too late. When she tilted the envelope, at least twenty large-print photographs cascaded across the surface. The array of pictures were of Andrea and Kathy, crying, smiling, and arguing. In the last few, Kathy held Andrea's hand, and it looked as if she was stroking over the back of Andrea's hand with her thumb.

A cough from the doorway startled her out of her disbelief. She glanced at Michael's tired, bleary face.

"Good morning," she choked out, her voice betrayed her emotions. She was trying so hard to stop herself from being sick.

Ambling into the kitchen, his hands tucked deeply in the pockets of his midnight blue silk robe, he stood next to her and gazed at the scattered pictures. He mouthed *what the fuck*, but no sound followed.

"Put those away and come on outside and have a smoke. We need to talk."

***

Circumstance
Kate Charlton

Helen huddled against the cold in a padded coat, her hand trembling as she lifted the cigarillo to her lips and inhaled deeply. The first lungful gave her a tobacco head-rush that relieved her tension just enough to think straight. Michael watched her wordlessly until he was satisfied that the shock had worn off. Tendrils of cigarette smoke wafted up into the still air as he spoke.

"They met on Friday at a café in town because Kathy had quite a few questions that she couldn't ask you. Your sister-in-law seems to have quite a big mouth after a few drinks." His quiet tone still held an air of disgust as he blew out a puff of smoke.

Helen bit her lower lip and took another drag on her cigarillo. "She told Kathy about us, didn't she?"

"The fact that Kathy is still here with you shows just how much she loves you, Helen. I think she's just incredibly hurt that you've kept such a huge part of your life from her. If it'd been a random stranger, then sure, maybe there'd be no reason to say anything, but your own sister-in-law whom you see all the time? Are you surprised she's freaking out and questioning whether this whole relationship is built on a lie?"

Shaking her head vehemently, Helen stubbed the smoke out in the ashtray.

Circumstance
Kate Charlton

"Oh, god, I love her and I want to spend the rest of my life with her. I didn't keep quiet about the affair because I still have romantic feelings for Andrea. I kept quiet because of the guilt and, quite frankly, embarrassment I feel about it. It was better to keep it quiet. If my brother found out, it would've ripped the whole fucking family apart." Her heart hammered in her chest. This was not how she'd envisioned her and Kathy's first Christmas.

"So, why did it end? Who ended it?" Michael probed gently.

She thought back to the darkest time in her life, almost a year ago, when her family had pulled her back from the brink of oblivion and took her to stay with them. It was a life-altering time for her. She'd been consumed by Meg's death and the months that followed were bleak.

David was working the weekend shift and the kids were out with Andrea's sister and her kids for a pantomime and pizza afternoon, which left them alone in the rambling house. She remembered how the touch of her lover's skin had tickled something deep inside her, a part of her that she thought had died along with Meg. Andrea had felt it at the same time and shuffled onto her lap, smothering her with deep, hungry kisses. Before they knew it, they'd landed in Andrea's bed where they'd ended up so many times before and made love for the final time.

She'd broken down in tears afterwards, letting Andrea rock her gently in her arms until the sobs finally subsided. Without ever saying a word, they knew it was over between them. So many things had changed since they'd first met and their relationship had finally reached its natural conclusion.

He listened patiently as she regaled the story, nodding from time to time. When she was finished, and tears streamed down her cheeks, he wiped them away with the sleeve of his coat.

"Come on, let's enjoy our Christmas and we can worry about all of this later. You know you're going to have to talk to Kathy about it sooner rather than later, right?"

With a deep breath, she nodded and pulled the big man into a hug, the solid strength of his body bringing her comfort. She'd be glad to start this day over again.

***

The cosy house bustled with noise as the kids chased the old dog around the garden whilst the adults sat in the kitchen, working their way through dinner and several bottles of wine.

Circumstance
Kate Charlton

Helen felt blessed as she watched Kathy, Andrea, and Paul work in perfect rhythm to peel vegetables, prepare tins of hot goose fat for roast potatoes, and make stuffing from scratch. She gulped back her drink and examined the two women. No one would have guessed that there'd been tension between them or a shared secret that had the power to rip the family apart.

"Have we got more wine?" she asked her brother with more joviality than she felt.

He slid his large frame off the stool and strode to the wine rack, examining the treasures it held with wide-eyed excitement. "White or red?"

"Red, I think, please. Never a good idea to mix when it's an all-day event."

"A marathon, not a sprint!" Michael agreed, holding his empty glass aloft.

As he pulled out a bottle, David examined the label, squinting to examine the small print. "How about a nice Cotes du Rhone reserve from 2012?"

"Perfect, but sip, don't gulp; it's an expensive bottle."

Like a pro, he uncorked it, filling their three glasses before asking the others what they wanted. He topped up

Andrea's glass, pecking her on the lips as he did so, which earned him a warm smile.

As Helen moved around them towards the oven, she could see Kathy's response to the interaction. She seemed devoid of emotions, but when she threw the vegetables into the pot a little harder than expected, Helen wondered if it was anger or repulsion that fuelled the spark of fire she'd seen in her eyes.

Will she leave me over this?

She slugged her wine and rolled her shoulders. "Okay, brace yourselves! Once everything's in pans and in the oven to cook, we're all heading out into the garden for Christmas rugby!" Cheers erupted from those who were used to this tradition.

When she didn't see Kathy smile, she crossed the kitchen and wrapped her arms around her waist and kissed her cheek. Kathy tensed, then relaxed. Helen heard her sigh.

"Christmas rugby, really?" she laughed.

Helen gave a lazy grin in response. "It's the only way to work up an appetite!"

The physical contact with her partner's body was the only thing that pushed the dread back down into the pit of her stomach. Helen feared that every moment without Kathy in her arms was a moment closer to losing her, and it drove her crazy.

***

The stillness of the early afternoon was broken as the six adults and two children marched out into the garden, chattering excitedly as Helen held a small, soft rugby ball aloft. She shouted out the rules above the noise. The children bounced around. Helen and Kathy were voted team captains and each chose their mates: Helen, Michael, Andrea, and Tom on one team, Kathy, David, Paul, and Hannah on the other.

Racing across the lawn, Kathy felt her legs go out from under her as strong arms grabbed her around the waist and sent her face-first into the cold, powdery snow. She lost sight of the ball as the warm body on top of her moved slightly and Andrea's cultured voice whispered "Sorry about that" against her ear. A shiver of warmth ran through her as she took the offered hand and allowed herself to be pulled back up. She couldn't look at her as she dusted the snow off her clothes and started to jog back towards her teammates.

After an hour of rough-housing, the family trooped back into the house, toasty warm despite the winter chill beyond its doors. It was a Christmas like none of them had had before, and one that they were very unlikely to forget.

Chapter 27

In the shadowy tree-line, still as a lioness stalking her prey, Petra hid, but she was close enough to the house to see into the lamp-lit living room. The vertical blinds partially obscured her view. She could just barely spy Helen seated by the fire, and the backs of two heads peeking above the sofa. A tiny shiver of anticipation ran down her spine.

The falling snow clung to her long woollen coat and settled in her hair. The nerves on the back of her neck twitched, and the white heat of anger burned inside her chest as the chocolate box vision of the perfect Christmas played out. If her life hadn't made a U-turn, she would be enjoying the holiday with Anna instead of being hundreds of miles away.

Stepping forward, her black hiking boots in line with the shadows, she unbuttoned her coat. Inside the ripped lining, she felt cold metal against her hand, then pulled out a heavy air rifle—complete with scope and silencer. The wooden stock felt good in her hands, smooth and cool against her skin as she raised the weapon to her shoulder. Through the scope, she saw her target. At first, she paused, steadied her hand. Then she pulled the trigger.

Circumstance
Kate Charlton

The sound of hard puffs of air came from the barrel. She watched as the pellets shattered the window.

***

The window behind Michael and Paul exploded into thousands of tiny shards, showering them both. Before anyone could react, a second window crashed. Screams filled the air as everyone ducked, automatically covering their heads with their arms.

David sprang forward, grabbed his wife, and pushed her to the floor.

"Down, everybody, get down!"

Andrea sobbed beneath her husband, shouting for the children in the other room to stay put.

Just as Paul crawled into the hallway to go to the children, the pane of glass from the front door blew out above his head, sending diamond-shaped shards over him. Helen heard him let out a moan as glass cut into the backs of his hands like a million tiny razors.

Everyone yelled as David propelled himself across the room to turn off the lamp and Christmas tree lights while Michael called the police. Helen used her body to shield both Kathy and Andrea.

Circumstance
Kate Charlton

The blood rushed in Helen's ears as they all laid in the darkness. Her eyes were trained up to the window frame, looking for any sign of movement beyond. Time seemed to come to a standstill as a figure appeared by the trees, a rifle raised in the air. Instinctively, she threw herself on top of the two women she was trying to protect. Then, two muffled shots rang out. White hot pain seared through her back, leaving her unable to catch her breath. She couldn't move. She tried to stay alert, but the voices around her were fading into the distance. Her vision blurred and everything faded to black.

***

Petra ran through the snow-covered garden and out towards the road, then suddenly stopped when her mind registered the rifle was no longer in her hands. *Bloody hell, I must've dropped it after firing the last shot.* She looked over her shoulder and scanned the ground. It was dark, but on the snow-filled walkway, a long dark figure stood out. There was no going back for it. She'd seen her intended target go down.

Euphoria flooded her veins as she leapt into the car and gunned the engine, peeling away from the kerb as quickly as she could. It wouldn't be much longer before the roads were blocked off by the police. She was sure it would be too late: Kathy would be dead and there was nothing anyone could do. A manic laugh escaped her as she peeled down the deserted streets. It was over. She'd won.

***

Blue flashing lights lit up the night outside. Sirens wailed until several police cars spun to a halt on the tarmac.

"Stay with me baby, oh, god, stay with me!" Kathy begged Helen through her sobs.

She pressed down on the wound to try to make it stop bleeding. *What if she dies? I can't lose her!*

***

Curled up in the corner of a lumpy, grey sofa in the ER waiting room, Kathy fixed her gaze on the magnolia wall ahead of her. Michael slumped in a chair opposite, whilst David paced the floor, shards of glass still glinting in his dark hair.

They'd sat for over an hour, waiting for news, wondering what was going on and why it was taking so long. Paul had driven Andrea and the kids home and agreed to stay with them.

Kathy smiled as she recalled the first time she and Helen met. If someone had told her then that she'd fall in love with a gorgeous, intelligent, sweet, lovable, and amazing woman on that holiday, she'd have called them crazy. Helen's eyes had drawn her in—bright, enigmatic.

She'd realised she loved her the minute she saw Althaia flirting with her in a way she'd obviously done many times before. Helen had become her shining light during her dark days. Yes, she could be a little short-tempered, yes, she had her faults and had kept secrets, but none of that mattered anymore. The fact that her lover's life was in danger both terrified her and made her realise that she needed to cherish what they had. She didn't want a life without Helen and didn't know how she'd cope without her.

The door opened and a young doctor entered the room, dressed in blue scrubs that were at least a size too large for his small frame. His identity badge hung from the waistband of his trousers. He stood in front of the door with a clipboard in his hands, commanding despite his stature.

"Hello, I'm Doctor Tariq Khan. Which one of you is next of kin for Helen Kennedy?"

Stepping forward, his shirt hanging loose from his trousers, David replied, "I'm her brother, but Kathy here," he turned and indicated with his hand, "is her partner. Helen would want her to be the first contact, I'd think."

With a nod, Doctor Khan waved his hand in a gesture for each of them to sit. He inhaled as he glanced at his notes.

"Doctor Kennedy was hit twice in the kidney with two pellets from a high-powered air rifle. Due to the angle of the shot, the rounds didn't hit bone, which would have deflected them and stopped them from causing further damage. During the CT scan, we've noticed a clot around her right kidney. Unfortunately, the only way we can treat this is through surgery." Pausing, he made eye contact with each of them, making sure that they understood what he was saying. "I'm quite confident that her kidney will heal well once we remove the object, but surgery of any kind carries some risks."

David pulled Kathy close and kissed her temple, as though he was somehow able to read her mind.

"This isn't your fault!" he whispered huskily into her ear.

With a sympathetic smile, Doctor Khan carried on, "The success rate of such an operation is very high, and Helen is likely to make a full recovery. We'll come and get you when she's being taken to the theatre and you can follow her up or head for home, whichever you prefer to do."

David and Michael stood and shook the doctor's hand, thanking him for his time and care. Kathy remained on the sofa, trying to process the information she'd just been given. In that moment, fear and rage swarmed her mind. All she wanted to do was find Petra Smythe and kill her with her bare hands.

***

Sitting on a bench in the middle of an enormous park, surrounded by layers of untouched, pure white snow, Helen looked out over an icy lake and a single gull flying high above bare trees. Her breath steamed out in front of her, but she wasn't cold. Fingers wrapped around hers.

"Is it time to go?" she asked, not needing to look to see who was beside her.

Meg leaned in close, the thin fabric of her linen shirt revealing the smoothness of her skin. "No, my love, your life is just beginning. This is just a stop-off, if you like. A chance to take stock of your life."

Helen watched the seagull as it traced through the sky above the trees. "So why are you here?"

"To make sure you don't make the same mistakes again. To make sure you give it all you've got this time."

Her eyes burning with tears, Helen's words caught in her throat. "I always loved you."

Meg stroked her fingers through Helen's short, spiky waves, and replied gently, "I know you did, and I always loved you. You always were the love of my life, despite your faults, despite the times you broke my heart." Her voice trailed off and her gaze lowered to the ground. "I knew, but I loved you too much to let you walk away, so I kept quiet. Now you have Kathy, and this is your one true chance. You're the love of her life, so don't let her down. Give her what she deserves and put the past behind you. I always loved you, and I forgive you."

Helen turned and looked into those beautiful eyes as if for the first time.

"Just take care of yourself. Things aren't over yet. You need to take care of both of you." She lifted Helen's hand to her lips and kissed her palm before her gaze returned to the skies. "You need to go back now. Follow the gull; he's waiting to take you home."

Helen tried to reply but the words wouldn't come as Meg's image faded. She tried to reach out, tried to fight to get back to her, but it was futile. The world flashed

Circumstance
Kate Charlton

back into colour as her eyes flew open and a searing pain burned through her stomach, into her back. Kathy's concerned face hovered above her.

Circumstance
Kate Charlton

Circumstance
Kate Charlton

Chapter 28

"You're awake!" Andrea whispered, a genuine smile brightening her tired face as she placed her hand over Helen's. Helen blinked rapidly to clear the grit from her eyes. Kathy... Kathy had been here. What had happened?

"Where's Kathy?" Helen croaked. "I need..." She pointed to her throat and let out a dry cough.

Andrea reached over to the water pitcher and poured the contents into a glass, then placed the rim of the cup to Helen's lips. "She's at our place. I made her go home to get some rest. It's just after seven in the evening on Boxing Day, and she's been by your side since you were brought in last night."

"What the hell happened? And why do I have an overwhelming urge to pee?"

Andrea stood and stretched her long limbs. "You were shot twice in the back with a high-powered air rifle by Psycho Almighty. One of them hit your kidney, unfortunately, and you have a catheter in, so don't worry about needing to pee."

She groaned in frustration as she struggled to get comfortable.

"Kathy's okay," Andrea added gently. "Your windows are getting replaced tomorrow, and the boys are there in the meantime taking care of the place. As for that psycho bitch, she's disappeared again."

Helen felt as though she'd been dragged into a horror film and she didn't know if she had the energy to fight her way out anymore. She let her head drop back onto the pillow and scrunched her eyes closed.

"I just need to get out of here. Kathy and I have some talking to do, and this woman needs to be caught."

With her eyes cast down and her shoulders slumped, Andrea took her hand. "You're not breaking up with her, are you?"

"Of course not. I need to talk to her about you and I. I know she knows, and I need to address it before it tears us apart."

"I'm sorry. I didn't mean for any of this to happen."

"I know." Helen had been ready to yell at her for telling Kathy, but when Andrea rocked on her heels and gazed around the room, Helen inhaled and looked away.

***

Petra hadn't taken any chances following the shooting and had driven straight back to London to hide out in her flat for a while. The elation of her achievement had worn off halfway through the drive, replaced by a feeling of utter exhaustion. To keep herself awake, she'd replayed her adventure. She loved the way the windows had exploded as she shot them out, the screams that came from the house, and the feeling of complete control as she fired off two shots into Kathy's back. She'd deliberately aimed for soft tissue, knowing that the pellets would only bounce off bone. Being with Anna was nearly within her reach. She could almost smell her all-too-familiar perfume and feel her touch. Tingles of excitement and anticipation ran through her body, rejuvenating her again.

Sleep claimed her the moment she fell onto her bed fully-clothed, and she drifted off into darkness.

***

Helen and Kathy spent an entire afternoon talking about things that Helen should have revealed months ago. They cried, laughed, and held each other on the hospital bed that Helen was so desperate to escape from. The sheets itched, and the plastic mattress made her hot and sticky. She wasn't a woman who was used to being immobilised. It made her twitchy and frustrated.

Kathy pushed herself up onto her elbow and regarded her, a concerned frown creasing her brow. "Does something hurt?"

Circumstance
Kate Charlton

Helen's dry throat made her cough, causing a stab of white-hot pain to shoot through her back.

"It didn't!" she snapped.

Kathy slid from the bed and stood awkwardly, hugging her arms tightly around her chest. "I'm sorry."

With a roar of frustration, Helen pounded the mattress several times as she laid her head back against the pillow. Lashing out was the only way to vent her anger and frustration at the situation she found herself in.

"You know what?" Helen's voice sounded as rough as gravel, and Kathy's eyes snapped open. "This isn't just about you, for fuck's sake! You don't get a monopoly on being the victim here!"

She looked over. It was as though a stranger had invaded Kathy, turning her into a shaking, enraged crazy woman. Her wide eyes looked almost black as tears shone at the edge of her lids, her cheeks a flaming red. Helen shrank back in the bed.

Kathy's voice came out in heaving sobs, her gaze fixed firmly on the ceiling. "I thought you were going to fucking die! All through Christmas after I'd found out about you and Andrea, I was wondering how long it would take you to come clean, to admit what you'd both done." Kathy glared at her, and her stomach dropped. She looked away, unable to meet that fiery gaze. "Were you ever going to tell me?"

Helen licked her dry, cracked lips and fought back the nausea that gripped her.

"Yes, I was going to tell you, sweetheart. You have to believe me," she pleaded.

A moment passed between them, the silence stretching until it became uncomfortable. Kathy roughly wiped the tears from her face with the back of her sleeve and sniffed loudly. "I don't know what to believe anymore."

Helen tried to find words of comfort, something, anything, but she was rendered speechless as Kathy gave a sad smile and dug her hands into the pockets of her for-fitting jeans. She turned her gaze down to the floor, shoulders slumped in defeat, and strode out of the room.

"Kathy! Please come back. Don't leave me. Jesus!" She struggled to try and pull herself around onto the side of the bed, but another explosion of pain stopped her. Helen fell back against the pillows, feeling as though her world was crashing down around her.

***

Circumstance
Kate Charlton

Sprawled on her old leather sofa, Petra lit another cigarette and blew smoke rings into the air, captivated by the way the fragile silver circles dispersed into nothingness. It was a trick her father had performed, and she had refused to leave him alone until he told her how it was done. With a thin smile, she recalled how her mother had managed to spoil those moments, too, admonishing him for encouraging a small girl to smoke.

Petra snapped back into the present, glancing at the packets of biscuits, crisps, ice cream, and a large bottle of cola all empty on the coffee table. She picked up her phone to scour the local news. Butterflies took flight as her gaze fell upon a headline that described her very own little Christmas party.

Prominent Newcastle GP's Home Attacked by Gunfire on Christmas Day

Dr. Helen Kennedy was attacked in her home at 20.15 hrs on Christmas Day after celebrating with her family. The 39-year-old found herself under fire when the windows on the ground floor of her home were shot out by an intruder wielding a powerful airgun in an attack that police have described as "despicable".

Dr. Kennedy was shot twice in the back during the attack but is currently recovering in the hospital. No one else was injured during the shooting.

Circumstance
Kate Charlton

Detective Inspector Ian Fletcher of Northumbria Police has asked for anyone with information about the crime to come forward and help with their enquiries.

Bile rose in her throat as her heart pounded in her ears. A roar of pure rage shattered the silence as she launched the phone across the room. The device smashed into pieces as it hit the wall, chunks of plastic and glass littering the worn carpet. Petra upended the table as though it was as light as air and swiped the books from the shelf on the corner cabinet. The roaring in her head was loud as a jet was flying too close to the ground. She slid down the wall, rocking slowly, knees pulled to her chest. Her glazed eyes stared at nothing. She'd shot the wrong woman, and that woman had survived.

***

Relief flooded through Helen as she opened her front door. After four days spent in the hospital enduring a catheter, she was glad to be out of there. Her back still ached badly, and she still needed the pain relief meds, but she refused to take the full dose because they turned her into a zombie.

Though she hadn't seen or heard from Kathy, she knew she hadn't returned to London, thanks to Andrea and David's reassurances. It did nothing to stop the heavy sense of dread that clutched at her heart like an iron fist.

Circumstance
Kate Charlton

She'd spent her nights in the hospital tossing and turning, wondered if the damage done to their relationship was irreparable.

Standing in the hallway, leaning heavily on the staircase rail, Helen listened for any sounds that would tell her Kathy was home, but none came. Behind her, David bustled through the door with her overnight bag slung over his shoulder and stopped beside her, noticing the look of panic on his sister's fine-boned features.

"Come on, let's get you into the front room so you can get your feet up and relax like you've been told."

He dropped the bag by the coatrack with a heavy thud and steered her through the doorway with a little push before beating a hasty retreat to the kitchen.

Kathy lay on the sofa, her face turned towards the dying embers of the fireplace, peacefully asleep. Helen's breath caught in her throat, struck by the realisation of just how beautiful her lover truly was.

Desperate not to disturb her, she tiptoed across the room and knelt in front of her. Beautiful. The tiny lines around her eyes, the fullness of her lips, and the flecks of silver that decorated her perfect auburn curls. Helen couldn't help but reach out and push a stray lock of hair away from Kathy's forehead.

Circumstance
Kate Charlton

Long, dark eyelashes fluttered open. Kathy gave a small smile and reached for the hand that rested on her cheek, pulling the palm to her lips.

"Welcome home," she whispered.

***

The aroma of fried onions filled the room. In the kitchen, Paul happily cooked omelettes as Michael made himself busy in the garden, topping up the bird feeders in the trees.

"How are you feeling?" Paul asked Helen.

"Better now that I'm home. I still ache a bit, and I'm knackered, but other than that…I'm so grateful to the two of you, you know?" She gestured towards the garden. "We couldn't have done any of this without you."

Paul draped an arm around her shoulder and pulled her close. "It's been our pleasure. You are two of our closest friends, so it goes without saying that we'll do anything to help. We're all just relieved that you're okay. What have the police said?"

With a deep sigh, she focused on filling the kettle from the tap and switched it on to make tea. "Well, the gun didn't have any prints on it because she wore gloves, though they did find footprints out in the treeline where she'd been standing. Evidence-wise, there isn't much, but we know it's her. They'll try to find out where the gun was purchased, which should be easy enough, but that's probably why she chose an air rifle. You don't need a license to get one."

High heels echoing on the tiled hallway floor signified Kathy's approach. She strode into the kitchen, her brow creased when she saw Helen in the kitchen helping.

Helen held her hand up to stop her before she could say anything.

"I'm fine! Movement is part of recovery, and if I sit much longer, I'll end up with a blood clot from immobility." She pulled Kathy into her arms and kissed her nose. "I love you very much, honey, but you need to let me breathe a little bit. Doctor, heal thyself and all that mumbo-jumbo."

"The doctor needs to take her own advice."

***

Helen did just that and took time to heal, working from her home office that she'd designed. Her favourite feature of the room was the double loveseat below the window, which was where she sat now, hugging a cup of hot milk and brandy close to her chest. The room was so unlike the rest of the house, with its polished oak flooring,

Circumstance
Kate Charlton

built-in ebony book cases and cabinets, and her favourite piece: the art deco style oak desk that she'd inherited from her father. Helen smiled fondly, remembering him working long hours at it as she'd sat across the room, doing her homework, and later, studying for university. She missed him greatly.

A knock on the door pulled her back from her reverie.

"Come in," her voice cracked.

The door slowly creaked open and Kathy's dark curls appeared around the doorframe. She looked to Helen, a small smile brightening her beautiful face. "Are you okay?"

"I'm just having a bit of me time. Come and join me."

Kathy slid through the door, closing it behind her, and made her way to the loveseat where Helen leaned against the solid side of a bookcase. She took the warm hand offered to her, wrapping her fingers around the soft skin, and allowed herself to be pulled down onto the sofa.

Without a word, Helen wrapped her arm around her lover's shoulders and snuggled into her embrace.

Shutting her eyes, Kathy whispered, "I'm still hurt, and I'm still mad at you, but I do love you."

Circumstance
Kate Charlton

The snowfall beyond the window caught Helen's attention as she rested her chin on the top of Kathy's head. She tangled her fingers in the curls at the nape of her slender neck and sighed deeply. "And I love you. I know it's going to take time."

Silence hung between them and the tension became almost tangible as it crackled in the room. Kathy raised her head and opened her eyes. Kathy whimpered as their tongues met, tentatively at first, until the smouldering embers of pain burst into flames of wanton desire.

Circumstance
Kate Charlton

Chapter 29

Anxiously shifting her weight from foot to foot, Petra stood at the apartment's front door and knocked for the second time. She'd waited for a group of strangers to enter through the locked lobby and tagged onto the back of the trio, allowing her to gain access to the building.

She wasn't going to leave until she'd spoken to Anna. She bit at her thumbnail.

Anxiety washed over her at the metallic rattle of the safety chain and deadbolt being undone on the other side. The door opened slowly, silently, revealing a forty-something blonde with fine features and reading glasses perched on the edge of her nose. For a moment, Petra thought her heart would explode out of her chest now that they were face-to-face again. Then, just as suddenly, a zen-like calm descended over her.

***

Petra had been blonde when Anna had last seen her, and her hair had been longer, too. Now she had a short, dark bob and her face looked thinner, more angular, emphasising the hollows beneath her cheek bones.

Anna used her body to try and block the entrance to the apartment. She sucked in a deep breath.

"Petra! What the hell are you doing here?"

"Aren't you glad to see me, darling?" Petra asked, her head cocked to one side. A frown line creased her forehead.

Anna cast her eyes over the long coat, the low heels, the slim fitting black slacks and black cashmere sweater. "Why are you here?" She held the door firmly in her hand, ready to slam it if she had to.

"To see you, to sort everything out for us. We're free now. That lawyer bitch isn't going to come between us anymore. I made sure of that." Her smile was lopsided as she bit again at the jagged thumbnail.

"You shot her girlfriend, Petra! What the fuck kind of person goes around shooting people? You're fucking crazy!" Her voice vibrated off the hallway walls.

The smile slid from Petra's features and her eyes blazed like fire. She forced the door open and wedged it with her foot so Anna couldn't close it. Anna backed up as Petra strode into the hallway and slammed the door, blocking her only escape route.

Circumstance
Kate Charlton

"I did it for us." Her words were slow and menacing as she marched past her towards the lounge area.

Lacing her hands behind her head, Anna tried to rationalise. "Petra, you have to listen to me. You and I haven't been together in over four years, and then you stalked my ex-girlfriend to the point that she almost had a nervous breakdown. I should have stopped you then, but I was too self-absorbed and scared of losing what I had. There is no *us*. There never really was."

***

Petra stopped and picked up a black-and-white photograph in a plain silver frame. It was a picture of Anna and Kathy, taken several years ago at a party. She knew that because she'd been there. It'd been a work event where the champagne had flowed freely, and she hadn't taken her eyes off her lover as she'd played the good wife with Kathy.

She ran a finger over the two faces in the snapshot before throwing it to the floor. Petra swallowed back the bile that rose, satisfaction warming her insides as the glass shattered into tiny pieces and the frame broke apart.

***

Circumstance
Kate Charlton

Anna flinched at the sudden aggression and the noise of the impact. She didn't dare speak; instead, she pushed her hands deeply into her pockets.

Turning back to face Anna, the smile returned to Petra's face. "I know she's got to you. Can't you see that she's trying to keep us apart? That fucking bitch walked out on you when she found someone else." She stepped closer and tried to take Anna in her arms.

She reeled back in disgust. "You need help. You're sick." Abhorrence dripped from her words.

"Don't you fucking dare!" Petra spat. "I've done everything for you, I fought for you, and what do I get? I get nothing but shit!" Her nostrils flared before her mood and demeanour instantly changed again. "Come on, baby, remember all the good times we had? Extravagant hotel rooms with the best champagne, mind blowing sex that lasted all night long. Surely you can't have forgotten all of that?"

Anna didn't respond. Her heart beat frantically in her chest. Petra was insane, and arguing facts was getting her nowhere. She turned on her heels, sat on the sofa, and tucked her feet beneath her. "I'm sorry, it's just been so long since we've seen each other, and you stayed away for so long. It's just a surprise to see you again. I didn't mean to sound so abrupt or cruel. And you're right. Kathy is a bitch, and she deserves all she gets. I just need some time to get used to having you around again. I've missed you."

***

It had been a long week, so before the drive back to London, Helen and Kathy spent time alone to talk and get their lives back on track. Kathy insisted since she needed to return to work. Their lives were once again going to change.

Turning to observe Kathy's profile, Helen admired how the sun accentuated the contour of her cheekbones.

"What are you thinking?" Kathy asked without looking at her.

"How much I'll miss you when you're back in London."

Kathy ran her thumbs over the soft leather covering the steering wheel and sighed.

"I know, I've been thinking about when you got shot…." Her voice caught in her throat. "it scared the shit out of me and it made me realise that I'd be lost without you. We've both been through so much shit over these past few months and that's even encroached on my work life. Even though the allegations she made against me were false, people still look at me differently and I can't bear that. So maybe now is the right time to be looking for a new job: closer to you and away from London."

A smile pulled at the corner of Helen's mouth. "As in, move in with me? Move to Newcastle?" She sounded like an excited child.

"Yeah, as in, make a life with you. Finally. One thing I learned through all the drama: we can get through anything together."

"Does that mean I'm forgiven?"

Kathy licked her lips and smirked. "Forgiven, yes, but forgetting... I'm not sure I'll ever be able to do that. There's a saying that the Japanese fix their broken objects by filling the cracks with gold. Because if something with history has suffered and been damaged, it can become more beautiful. The gold is always going to remind you of the damage, but it becomes a part of the object. I really do believe that relationships are like that." She reached for Helen's hand and squeezed her fingers tightly.

"I promise to never keep anything from you again."

Kathy leaned further back in her seat. "I'll hold you to that."

***

Circumstance
Kate Charlton

After Petra finally left, Anna huddled in the corner of her sofa for a long time, trying to stop the shaking that'd overcome her body. Petra left after Anna promised to meet with Kathy and tell her that they were seeing one another again. She hadn't thought that the deranged woman would fall for it, but she had.

When she managed to pull her phone out of her pocket, she called the police and reported that Petra Smythe had been there. The next number she tried to call was Kathy's, but the number was no longer in service. Anna growled in frustration and jumped up from the sofa, pacing the floor as she tried to think. She had no idea what to do. She needed to warn Kathy. She owed her that much. Without further thought, she slid on her jacket and raced out of the apartment, vowing that Petra Smythe wasn't going to dominate their lives anymore.

***

Traffic across London was slow in the period between Christmas and New Year as bargain hunters descended on the sales racks. Petra honked her horn. Other motorists did the same, and before long, frustrated drivers yelled out their windows.

There was no use getting angry. No matter how long she had to sit there, she was on top of the world. Anna had just agreed to give Petra her heart. All of it. All the hard work and effort she'd put in over the past few years was finally paying off. Getting rid of Kathy Harland was the best decision she'd ever made. Her gut feeling told her that the bitch would probably be back in London by now, though she didn't know why. The only way she'd know for sure was by dropping by her place and watching for a while to see who came and went.

Petra remembered the first time she'd seen Kathy. It was just before the company Christmas party. She knew Anna was with her, but until she was forced to come face-to-face with her nemesis, she'd never thought of her as a threat. The next day, she begged Anna to be her date for the company event. Anna backtracked, giving her a handful of reasons why she couldn't. It infuriated her that Anna was bringing Kathy, but she had no say. However, she was dead-set on making sure that Anna wouldn't be able to take her eyes off her all night. Dressed in a low-cut cocktail gown, she had positioned herself at the bar, providing her with a perfect view of the entrance.

The moment Anna appeared, Petra's breath caught in her throat. The beauty before her had been dressed in a black gown that lay delicately against her hourglass figure. Her excitement faded when Kathy appeared beside her in a long, midnight-blue strapless dress with a matching bolero jacket.

Circumstance
Kate Charlton

She'd waited until they got to the bar before making a move, pushing past a young guy to ensure her ability to stand next to Anna.

"Going to buy a girl a drink?" she'd asked huskily.

Anna's lip curled up as she turned to face her. Petra could see Anna was not happy with her, but she didn't care. Whether Anna liked it or not, she was going to introduce her to Kathy

Instead of cowering down and making light of the introduction, Anna smiled, slipped her hand into Kathy's, and introduced her as her fiancé. Petra felt a knot form in the pit of her stomach. Her voice failed her, but her mind screamed loud in her ears. That was when everything changed. Anna started to make excuses about why they couldn't see one another, and eventually broke it off.

Circumstance
Kate Charlton

Chapter 30

Despite the cold outside, Kathy threw open the patio doors that led out onto the balcony, allowing the cool fresh air in to flush out the stale smell of an unlived-in home. She wasn't looking forward to emptying her suitcase, but she had no choice. Another bonus of moving to Newcastle: no constant to-ing and fro-ing with her belongings.

Lounging on the sofa, Helen tried not to laugh at the way Kathy ran around.

"Why don't I make us a hot cup of tea, honey?" she called out.

"You know what? That would be wonderful and just what I need right now!" Kathy popped around the doorframe and grinned.

Easing herself up from the sofa, Helen made her way towards the kitchenette, humming as she filled the kettle and got two mugs from the cupboard. Her body still ached but she was feeling stronger every day.

***

Circumstance
Kate Charlton

Within minutes of parking near the apartment building, Petra noticed the patio doors were open and Kathy was clearly talking to someone else inside. *The good doctor*, she surmised. Her hunch had been right, and she felt strong enough to take on both if she needed to. She couldn't imagine Helen being fully recovered from her injuries, so she would be the easiest one to take out first. *How will Kathy react to watching her new girlfriend die?* She laughed to herself, imagining them both begging for their lives, pleas that would fall on deaf ears.

A short while later, Petra sat to attention as the underground private garage doors opened and Kathy's car inched out. But it wasn't Kathy driving, it was Helen. Her prayers appeared to have been answered and she whooped loudly, realising that her mission had been made a whole lot easier. One at a time was all the sweeter, and the doctor could wait until later.

***

Seeing the tail-lights of Kathy's car as it pulled out of the parking garage, Anna accelerated away from the apartments. She cursed loudly and considered her options for a second before deciding to follow her.

***

Circumstance
Kate Charlton

Helen switched the radio on and whistled along to Springsteen as he sang "Growing Up in America". The snow hadn't hit London the same way it had Newcastle and Helen was glad the roads were clear as she drove. She glanced in the rear-view mirror and noticed that a cherry red Range Rover Sport had been behind her since she left the apartment. She couldn't see the driver due to the sun visor being pulled down, but something told her that things weren't right. She pressed the accelerator a little harder to put some distance between her and her new unwelcome friend, checking the mirror every couple of seconds. She had no idea what kind of car Petra Smythe drove, but she wouldn't be surprised if the crazy woman had decided to finish what she'd started.

When the Range Rover caught up, Helen felt her heart beat faster in her chest. She checked the traffic around her and swung a sharp left into the first side street. Sure enough, the sporty number spun around the corner after her and Helen felt as though she'd suddenly been thrown into an action movie. She tried to concentrate on the road and prayed that she wouldn't get killed in this craziness. Her hands felt clammy. How many times could she cheat death?

Helen was sure she was dreaming. Things like this didn't happen to normal, everyday people, and yet here she was, driving through the streets of London heading god-only-knew-where to escape. The whites of her knuckles were visible on the steering wheel; it had to be Petra Smythe following her and she was terrified that this time, she'd finish what she'd started. She sped through an amber light and took a hard right, not having any idea where she was headed but knowing that she had to break away and get back to the apartment. All she could think about was getting back to Kathy and making sure she was okay.

***

Anna's tires screeched on the asphalt as she followed the smaller car around yet another bend. These cars weren't exactly designed for tailing or keeping up with others on the streets of London. Why the hell was Kathy doing this? She wasn't a threat. She was trying to save her goddamned life, but all she was getting was the slip, as though Kathy was afraid of her. She'd made some catastrophic errors in their relationship, but she'd never, ever physically hurt her. Anna was trying to protect her. If it was the last thing she ever did for the woman she loved and then lost, it had to be done properly.

***

The buildings blended into one as they raced past the houses. Helen pushed well past the speed limit. There was a busy road up ahead. She stomped on the brakes as hard as she could and braced her body, but her reactions were too slow: she overshot the give way-markings and ploughed into the oncoming traffic. A van smashed into the side of the car in a screech of tearing metal and a hiss of bursting radiators. The air bag deployed into Helen's chest and her world once again faded to black.

***

Petra was always amazed at how entirely stupid apartment security people were. She'd used her age-old trick of sliding through behind someone else and wasn't even acknowledged by the guy on the desk. She'd smiled to herself all the way up in the lift, her thumb stroking over the smooth handle of the eight-inch chef's knife she'd strapped to her leg beneath her coat. Today was going to be a good day.

Tap, tap.

Her knuckles rapped against the oak door. She could hear music playing loudly and knocked again. After a few seconds, a voice called out from the other side.

***

Kathy opened the door. She gasped and stepped back, and the heel of her slipper caught onto the hallway rug, causing her to stumble. Petra strode in just as she had at Anna's, only this time, she didn't say a word. She used the heel of her shoe to kick the door shut with a satisfying thud and appraised the décor as though she were a prospective tenant.

Her hands buried deeply in the pockets of her frock coat, Petra nodded slowly.

"Nice place you've got here. Shame the security is so abysmal."

"Why are you here?" Kathy's voice was barely a whisper.

Making herself comfortable on the sofa, Petra crossed one long leg over the other.

"I knew she'd take her time coming to see you. Anna, that is. So I thought I'd save a little bit of time and come to see you myself."

With extreme reluctance, Kathy perched on the edge of the other sofa beyond the coffee table before her legs gave way under her. "What has that got to do with me?"

Petra's bitter laugh held no trace of humour. "Because you are the one person who's stood in our way for all this time. She and I could've been together years ago, but you, you selfish little bitch, weren't willing to let her go. You didn't want her, any fool could see that, but you weren't willing to let her be happy with anyone else, either." Her voice became harder the longer she spoke.

"I asked you. What does that have to do with me?"

Ignoring the outburst, Petra rolled her eyes and continued, "I remember when I first saw you. I just knew the pair of you weren't right together. Anna was classy and refined, but you, you just looked like a leech who clung to her for all she could get." She spat the words, her eyes remaining fixed beyond the window. All the while, her fingers fiddled with the buttons on her coat.

Kathy's gaze darted around the room.

"She was already in love with me then," she carried on, her voice taking on a dream-like quality. "She'd spent nights in my arms, booked us into hotel rooms for long lunches, and made love to me. I gave her what she wanted, what she needed. I gave her the love and attention that she craved. Not like you! All you were interested in was your own fucking career and using her money to move you on to better things."

"Petra, I…" Kathy began.

Petra exploded to her feet and overturned the heavy table as though it was made from cardboard. "Shut up, you bitch! I'm fucking talking!"

Circumstance
Kate Charlton

***

Anna yanked hard at the car door. She frantically yelled for help to the emergency services on the other end of the phone. The driver of the van had suffered only minor cuts and scratches, but the woman in Kathy's car was slumped behind the wheel with a visible head wound. The passenger door wouldn't give, and Anna was terrified that the woman inside would die if she couldn't get to her.

People appeared from all directions, some to gawp, some to try and help. Two men approached the car and told her that the only way in was to smash out the window. Anna stood back as the taller of the two booted the glass until it gave way, but both men were too big to fit through the gap. With their help, she wiggled through the ragged space, her cardigan catching on shards of glass. She clambered inside until her whole body was on the back seat. She scrambled to the woman and felt for a pulse.

"I have no idea what your name is, but I'm here to help you, and by god, you'd better not give up on me! Kathy would fucking kill me!"

***

After plucking a bottle from the wine rack in the kitchen, Petra helped herself to a glass. She wandered

Circumstance
Kate Charlton

around the place as though it was her own and she had every right to be here, every right to help herself to anything she wanted, as Popolo di Pekino swelled from the stereo.

Frozen in place, Kathy watched on as Petra made herself comfortable on the other sofa nearest the patio doors, the kitchen knife resting in her lap like it was the most normal thing in the world. She noticed how blank and devoid of emotion the woman seemed. If she didn't know better, she would have sworn that Petra was soulless.

"Why did you do it?" she asked after a long, heavy silence. "Why did you keep her away from me?"

No matter what she said, Kathy knew that there wasn't going to be a right answer here.

"I didn't even know about you until this year, when Anna and I split up. I wouldn't have known about you at all had you not terrorised me for the past few years." She knew the reply was antagonistic, but she couldn't help herself. This woman had spent over four years trying to destroy her life.

Petra's gaze landed on her, her eyes appraising every inch of her tense body. "She was always afraid you'd take her for all she had. Every last penny. I knew you had a hold on her and that was why you wouldn't let her come to me, no matter how hard she tried. Did you think she really loved you?" Her laugh was shallow, humourless. "It was me she made love to, me she whispered those three little words to. Do you really think she had any thoughts of you when she'd been in my bed, inside me?"

The question sounded rhetorical and Kathy didn't know what to say until Petra leapt forward and slammed the palm of her hand down on the table, wine sloshing out of the glass and over her hand, drops of it hitting the cream carpet like blood spatter.

"Did you, bitch?" she screamed.

Every inch of her skin prickled with fear and she fought the urge to vomit.

"N-no," Kathy stammered.

Oh, God, where's Helen? She should be back by now! She'd lost track of time but it felt as though she'd been trapped here with Petra for hours.

Pacing the living area, Petra held the knife down by her leg, almost as though she'd forgotten that she was carrying it. She examined rows of books and CDs, nodding occasionally as though she approved of what she was seeing. Kathy could see her shoulders rising and falling as she breathed deeply, but the rest of her body was as still, like a panther stalking its prey.

She wondered if she'd be able to make a run for it or at least grab something to use as a weapon, but again, there was nothing she could see. Her skin felt cold and clammy beneath her clothes and her stomach was knotted so painfully it hurt. She needed to try a different approach as the current one wasn't getting her anywhere.

"You don't need to be here to warn me off, Petra. I haven't seen Anna or heard from her in months. I'm not a threat to you and Anna. You can walk out of here now and we can forget that any of this ever happened."

Kathy wasn't sure that Petra had heard her as she continued to stand perfectly still, facing the bookshelf. It was a while before she broke into a menacing chuckle that chilled Kathy to the bone.

Petra turned slowly, her face contorted into a grin. Slowly, she stepped closer, her grip tightening on the knife.

"Oh, I know all about your new girlfriend," she spat. "I watched you once, through the window when you were too disgusting to even close the kitchen blinds. I saw what she did to you, how she fucked you and how you opened your legs and let her. Having a hold over one woman isn't enough for you, is it? Even though you were happy to let some other dyke fuck you, you still wouldn't let Anna come to me!" She waved the knife at Kathy, sunlight catching the reflective tip as though it was coated in diamonds.

Kathy closed her eyes and waited to feel the cold steel plunging into her. Her breathing turned ragged, and there wasn't a thing she could do to stop the tears that spilled down her cheeks. "Please, that's not what it's like. It's never been like that!" The silence became deafening as she opened her eyes and saw Petra's face only inches from hers. She could smell the wine on her breath and the bitter sharpness of her perfume. Was she going to kill her here, where she sat?

"Liar!" Petra spat, spinning on her heel and walking back towards the open bottle on the bureau where she'd left it.

Chapter 31

Petra's eyes held a faraway look as she began to pace, but Kathy could swear that she saw the madness that lurked behind them. The knife glinted menacingly as the fading sunlight cast long shadows across the room that'd now taken on an eerie glow.

"She loves me. She's always loved me. The plan was for her to come here and tell you that we're going to be together. I thought she'd be here by now. That's why I came. I wanted to hear her say it, see the look on your face when you found out." Her speech pattern was short and rapid, her sentences disjointed as though she was reading from a manual.

Kathy felt as though she could see reality slipping away from the woman before her. The cloak of insanity that hung over her had begun its descent. Her gaze was haunted and wild. It was clear that trying to rationalise wasn't going to work, but neither was sitting on the sofa waiting for Petra to make her next insane move.

As Petra became transfixed by the setting sun beyond the glass, Kathy gingerly got to her feet. The room was freezing cold from the open balcony door and her limbs were stiff because of it, but she stood to her full height without her uninvited guest noticing. Kathy wondered if she could get to the kitchen in time to arm herself. She'd need to rush past Petra and kick her legs out from under her.

Okay, Harland, time to stop thinking and take some action! She threw her upper body forward and grabbed the edge of the table with both hands. Using all her strength, Kathy kicked off her slippers and sprinted towards the kitchen, the sound of her heartbeat thudding in her ears as she moved.

Petra vaulted over the top of the table to grab Kathy before she could reach the back of the apartment. Her long legs allowed her to gain on the shorter woman easily and she rugby tackled her to the ground, the knife flying from her grip as she did so. "Nessun Dorma" began its slow opening in the background—the soundtrack to their battle.

Kathy hit the floor hard and felt the air leave her lungs. Petra landed on top of her first before momentum rolled her off. Her muscular arms, however, were still locked around Kathy's upper body, pinning her. Kathy kicked out behind her, trying to make contact with shins, knees, anything that would hurt if she delivered a blow in the right place.

Circumstance
Kate Charlton

None shall sleep! None shall sleep. You too, princess... Pavarotti's tenor filled the room.

Petra's panting breath was hot and sickly sweet beside Kathy's ear. Kathy pulled away, forced her arms up under Petra's, and grabbed a thumb. She yanked it back hard and heard the snap of the bone breaking. Petra screamed out in agony and her grip on Kathy loosened.

But the mystery of me is locked inside of me...

Desperately, she scrambled away, her sock-clad feet sliding on the wooden floor. Forcing herself upright, she tried to propel herself away quickly enough to reach the knife, but Petra was too fit, too young, and she gained on her again, knocking her out of the way as she swooped to the floor and grabbed at it with her uninjured hand. Kathy sprinted across the room, pieces of broken crystal biting through her socks and into her feet, but the adrenaline coursing through her veins blocked out any sense of pain. She made it as far as the bedroom door before Petra gained on her again, raising the knife high above her before bringing her arm down hard. Kathy ducked, but not before the blade caught her left arm, tearing through the bare flesh. She screamed, more from shock than pain. Blood began to run over her skin and drip to the floor. Petra's momentum sent her crashing through the bedroom door.

Circumstance
Kate Charlton

No one will know my name…

Kathy ran towards the patio doors, screaming her lungs out in the open air. She could hear Petra scrambling to her feet behind her and she threw herself out onto the balcony, losing her footing as she did so. She grabbed frantically on the handle to pull the doors closed behind her. She wasn't fast enough. Petra threw herself towards Kathy. Using both feet, Kathy kicked out, her heels making contact with the side of Petra's knee. She buckled and hit the ground, giving Kathy just enough time to pull herself up. She reached out for the door, but Patra pulled at her. Kathy purposely threw herself backwards, forcing Petra up against the balcony rail, causing her enough pain to loosen the grip.

Petra's legs went from under her and her body reeled back. Her face morphed from shock to disbelief as her arms flailed in mid-air. She fought to regain her balance, but it was futile.

And we will, unfortunately, have to die, die!

Standing frozen in place, Kathy held her breath as momentum forced Petra's torso over the rail and gravity took her past the point of no return.

A crash like a bomb going off sounded below her. As much as she didn't want to look, she knew she had to. She

Circumstance
Kate Charlton

braced herself against the rail and leaned over to the street below, where cars were parked in a neat line on the road. The piercing wail of a silver Jaguar's alarm blared in the early evening darkness as Petra Smythe lay sprawled on its caved-in roof, a pool of blood slowly seeping from her head in a dark halo.

The sob that wracked Kathy's body was the most inhuman sound she'd ever made. Her legs crumpled beneath her and she wrapped her arms over her head, rocking in anguish and disbelief as the realisation hit her. Petra Smythe was dead. After four-and-a-half years of terror at her hands, the nightmare was finally over, and she was free. She threw her head back and screamed just as a crack of lightning lit up the sky.

Circumstance
Kate Charlton

Chapter 32

The hours after Petra's death had been filled with chaos and confusion. Kathy had called the police herself once she'd regained enough composure to think straight, to take in what had happened, and only then did she realise that Helen still hadn't returned home. She had no idea how long it had been. Time had stood still and the afternoon's events may have lasted for an hour or twelve hours; she had no idea.

Michael arrived mere minutes before the police, his face ashen as he pulled her into an enormous bear hug. Kathy assumed that it was because of Petra's attack until he'd whispered into her ear, telling her that Helen was going to be okay. Her world crashed down for the second time in thirty minutes as the realisation hit her. She wasn't the only one who'd been to hell that afternoon.

Knowing that Helen had been involved in yet another serious incident pushed Kathy to the edge of insanity, especially as she couldn't go anywhere until she'd spoken to the police and they let her leave the apartment.

It took every ounce of Kathy's reserve to stay calm as she walked into Helen's hospital room. The sight of the woman she loved, her face covered in blood and her right leg in a hip-to-foot splint, was enough to make her crumble. The crash had left her with a fractured femur, a severe concussion, and a laceration that ran from her forehead to her ear. Falling to her knees at the bedside, Kathy finally lost it next to the unconscious woman. Only Michael's strong arms stopped her from melting down completely.

Circumstance
Kate Charlton

EPILOGUE

Fierce, white sunlight glinted on the crest of the waves, giving the impression that a million brilliant diamonds were washing onto the shore. Kathy stretched her tanned, toned legs out on the lounger and wiggled her toes, enjoying the warmth on her skin. The ocean had always been a place of comfort and contemplation for her, no matter which part of the world she was in.

The nightmares still chased her at night, hiding in her subconscious and waiting to pounce when she was at her most vulnerable. There were times when Kathy would swear Petra Smythe was still very much alive and after her, even though it had been a year and a half since her death. Even now, she'd get flashbacks of the black coat fluttering in the wind as Petra's body fell through the night, and the sound she made as she hit the car.

Kathy swallowed hard and closed her eyes, pushing away the memories. Therapy was helping, but she knew that things would never be the same again. Forcing herself back into the present, she sucked in a deep breath, letting the aroma of sea salt and nearby orchids calm her.

Strong fingers stroked through Kathy's curly ponytail and a cold drink was thrust into her hand. She looked up into Helen's face and felt an immediate tug of desire washing over her. "Mmm, thank you. What're we drinking?"

"Bloody Mary," Helen announced, hooking her walking cane over the spokes of the parasol.

"I do need something to cool me down. You're wearing me out this holiday," Kathy replied with a wink.

Helen gave a throaty laugh. Her gaze wandered over Kathy's bikini-clad body. "Can you blame me? A hot woman wearing very little, on the island where it all began. It's no wonder I can't get enough of you." Playfully, she waggled her eyebrows.

Sipping from her glass, Kathy raised an eyebrow over the rim. "You'd better drink up, Doc. I'm hungry, and I need something to sustain me before dinner."

That was apparently all the encouragement she needed. Helen drained her glass in three gulps and pulled herself to her feet.

"Let's go," she demanded.

***

Fresh seafood, Greek salad, and a platter of desserts had left them more than sated as they sipped on chilled white wine. Helen plucked a cigarillo from her tin and sparked it to life with a satisfied moan. It was one habit that Kathy had been unable to help her break, despite many protestations.

A familiar figure appeared by the table and paused, waiting for acknowledgement. It was Kathy who recognised the young Greek woman first.

"Althaia! You're still here!" She leapt to her feet and pulled the smaller woman into a hug, happy to see a familiar face.

"It's so good to see you both. I guess things are working out, yes?" She had such a beautiful smile.

Kathy blushed. It would take them forever to explain the events of the past two years. Instead, she held out her left hand, the thin gold band and diamond ring glinting on her finger.

With a gasp, Althaia covered her mouth with her hands and bounced on her feet. "Married?"

Reaching for her, Helen beamed. "Last week. She made an honest woman of me."

"I'm so happy for you! Both of you. Written in the stars, you see? Maybe my girl will pop the question soon enough."

Kathy took Althaia's other hand and grinned. "Tell us everything!"

"Well," she began, perching on a patio chair, "she holidayed here last year and she's from Germany. Older, a teacher, blonde. She stole my heart. I spent all of last winter with her in her country and she's been here this summer while I've come home to work. This will be my last season; I'm moving out there this year."

Helen suddenly realised how things had come full circle for all of them, and it made her heart swell with happiness. Everyone was content again: she and Kathy, Andrea and David, Althaia and her new love. Even Michael and Paul were starting to talk about walking down the aisle together.

Her attention was drawn to the skies as a plane flew overhead, coming in to land at the nearby airport. It made her think of her own flight to the tiny island two years ago, the journey that had introduced her to the love of her life.

Despite everything they'd been through, Helen Kennedy and Kathy Harland had made it, finding happiness in the craziest of situations.

"I wouldn't have it any other way," Kathy whispered to the stars.

THE END

Circumstance
Kate Charlton

Kate Charlton's Bio:

Kate originally comes from the small mining town of Consett, County Durham, but now lives in Middlesbrough with her partner, Karen. She's been an avid reader since discovering books in "infant school" and now reads everything from Vietnam War narratives to Lesfic.

When she's not stuck in front of a laptop, Kate spends her life as a qualified nurse, managing a dedicated team of women and men who dedicate their lives to others every day. Human nature is what makes her tick and she considers herself lucky to be in the privileged position of caring for others.

Since she was a teenager, Kate has written everything, from poetry to plays and novels, though this is her first foray into real writing since qualifying as a nurse twelve years ago. Fill her full of caffeine and she'll deliver anything you like! The spare time she has is spent indulging in cooking, family, playing bass guitar, and watching a good film.

Circumstance
Kate Charlton

Wicked Publishing books:

WICKED PUBLISHING BOOKS:

Hero by Ronni Meyrick

Absolute Betrayal by Ronni Meyrick

Shattering Rainbows by Ocean

Cricket by Barbara Dennis

A Wicked Anthology by Wicked Authors

Lioness by Kristen Kennedy

Pointless Resistance by HL Taylor

Serendipity by Aliyat Lecky

Circumstance by Kate Charlton

Flashback by Dawn Carter

Piece by Piece by Shiralyn J. Lee

Marine by Shiralyn J. Lee

Heartland by Vickie Adams

Saving Rainbow Falls by Leslie Foster Parker

Circumstance
Kate Charlton

Printed in Poland
by Amazon Fulfillment
Poland Sp. z o.o., Wrocław